N D

"As we move into a time when peace prevails on every continent and country, every home and heart, we are asked to evolve consciously. The women represented in this book have made that choice to see as God sees, feel as God feels and to know as God knows by sharing the stories of their divine missions."
‒ JAMES TWYMAN
Best selling author, musician and filmmaker

"This collection of stories from Evolutionary Women is a living 'chat room' offering new possibilities that inspire social pioneers to follow their souls' calling. Together, we can build a world of harmony, justice and beauty that reflects our highest potential and creates a pathway for future generations to flourish."
‒ CAROLYN ANDERSON
Co-author of *The Co-Creator's Handbook*

"Women telling stories: such an ancient manifestation of community. It evokes the warmth of campfires, of quilting bees, of family dinners. In the telling there is the acknowledgement of tattered lives. Yet there is also the weaving of the new, for these storytellers are women of today, with a long and broad view of what is needed to make the world a better place. The readers of this book are privileged to join this circle of Evolutionary Women who share their stories with the understanding that they are lovingly co-creating a new fabric of community that can hold and nurture us all."
‒ SUSANNE F. FINCHER
Author *Coloring Mandalas: For Insight, Healing, and Self-Expression*

"What a wonderful invitation to relate to the various parts in each of us as we read stories from our sisters. These are the stories needed as we learn to navigate our lives, to deepen our own experience of the divine feminine and masculine within us. I hope the reader will take time to write and reflect after each story: How is this like my own? What conscious choices will I make now?"
-- MARILYN ROSENBROCK NYBORG
Co-Founder, Gather the Women

"This book is a treasure for our times. Each chapter is a precious gem of women's wisdom exploring the deeply personal territory of bringing forth feminine leadership at this awesome moment in human history. The stories themselves are powerful; the fact that they came together in a fluid process, following a divine impulse with shared leadership, imbues the whole with an energy much more magnificent than the sum of its parts."
-- KATHE SCHAAF
Co-Founder, Gather the Women

"As you crawl into these pages know you are being embraced in an energy of divine feminine creation – the womb of a new emergence within the evolution of humanity. Invite yourself to be touched and changed by these incredible women—storytellers who will inspire you through their vulnerability and heartfelt desire to touch a part of you that is ready to give birth to an unseen potential beyond your current imaginings..."
-- REV. ANITA PATHIK LAW
Author, *The Power of Our Way: A Path to a Collective Consciousness*
www.powerofourway.com and www.divinitymovie.com

"*Conscious Choices* is truly a wonderful book filled with deeply touching true stories of spiritual transformations. The personal stories of the 44 women contributors bless and empower readers to become conscious of their own personal life story and myth. These are women who have discovered that a change for the better in their lives required their making a choice to change their consciousness; and that's exactly what they did. After reading *Conscious Choices* cover-to-cover, which I couldn't put down because it is filled with glorious stories of amazing and inspiring women, I felt a deep gratefulness to the Great Book Angels in my life that guide me to find books that are true blessings for my spiritual growth. *Conscious Choices* is an angelic blessing of the great book kind."

~ REV. JAYNE HOWARD FELDMAN
Author of *Commune with the Angels*; *Driving Under the Influence of Angels*; *Angels By My Side* www.earthangel4peace.com

"Stories of how a group of brilliant, dedicated women decided to make their lives count in building a positive future for the human family. They show how we bring our highest spiritual goals into the material world."

~ HAZEL HENDERSON
Author, *Ethical Markets: Growing the Green Economy*, co-author, *The Power of Yin*

"Co-creating is the new frontier, and now is the time for men and women together to weave a new partnership of equality and joy. The moving and powerful stories in this book show the way."

~ KATHLYN HENDRICKS
Co-author of *Conscious Loving and The Conscious Heart*

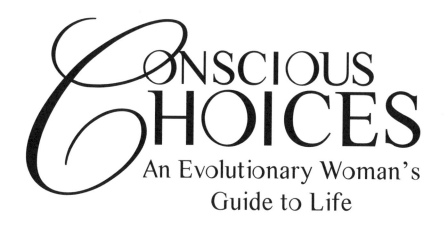

CONSCIOUS CHOICES

An Evolutionary Woman's Guide to Life

Love Your Life

Love Your Life Publishing
Dallastown, PA

Conscious Choices: An Evolutionary Woman's Guide to Life

Published by:
Love Your Life Publishing
PO Box 2, Dallastown, PA 17313
www.LoveYourLifeBooks.com

ISBN: 978-0-9798554-8-1
Library of Congress Control No: 2008941161

Cover design, layout and typesetting by
Cyanotype Book Architects
Editor: Judith Watson
Cover Photo by William McGowan

Printed in the United States of America
Printed on recycled paper.

A portion of the proceeds from the sale of this book will be
donated to further the work of Evolutionary Women.

Dedication

To those emerging as Evolutionary Women who courageously shared their stories in this book and to all the awakening women everywhere who have powerful stories to share.

Bonnie: To Sara, my ever-evolving daughter, her adventure-some husband Jeff, and my precious grandchildren, Maddy and Vinnie. To Brad Comann, my newly arrived Beloved, who showed up just in time for The Ultimate Celebration.

Lucky: To my sister, Franky Sweeny Helfrich, for all her love and support. To all the women I have loved and who have loved me, my life is graced through you.

Andrea: To my three Evolutionary daughters, Mary, Elizabeth and Hannah whose very presence on the planet inspired me to awaken the Evolutionary Woman who was hiding inside me.

Karen: For the beloveds in my life, my mother Oriole and grandmother Isabel for their love in the physical world and beyond, and to my husband David and sons, Anton and Sasha for their unwavering love and support.

A Blessing From

Her Holiness Sai Maa Lakshmi Devi

OM JAI SAI MAA

Beloved Souls, Embodiments of the Divine Feminine,

Remember that the evolutionary birthing of a new human being, a Divine Human Species of Light, is in the womb of woman. You have the power of creation in every cell, every molecule, every atom of your very Being.

Knowing that we embody the Divine Feminine Principle of Life itself, let us commit to greater Awareness, to more conscious choice of what we are creating.

As evolutionary women, we are vessels of knowledge, wisdom, grace, beauty, joy and Love. Let us embrace these qualities and together unify humanity and transform the universe.

I bow to your divinity. I bless your transformation. I pranam to the enlightened Being that you are.

With Great Love and Blessings,

Ever Yours,

Maa

Table of Contents

Part II: I Co-create with Others

Part III: I Express my True Self

Part IV: I Evolve my Relationships

Part V: I See a World that Works for Everyone

FOREWORD

Evolutionary Women

BARBARA MARX HUBBARD

Evolutionary Women of the world, greetings from one of your older sisters! I am here in Santa Barbara, sending my love and inspiration to each of you, and gaining strength from every one of you.

We are blessed to be born at this precise moment in evolution when the old world is dying and the new world is being born.

My sense is that Evolutionary Women are a vital part of that transition. There is encoded within us an emerging creativity that is vital to the future.

When we recognize ourselves as Evolutionary Women, something starts to change. Instead of getting older, we find we are getting newer every day. Why "new?" Because, the fact is, we have not seen the authentic feminine self fully present for thousands of years. Perhaps never before. For 5000 years patriarchal structures dominated most of the planet. Women could not possibly fully emerge. Now millions of us are free to express ourselves, for the good of ourselves and the whole human community.

Here is what I see is happening in our generation. The hierarchical, invisible social architecture that created civilization with all its magnificence and cruelty is no longer capable of handling the complexities of the emerging world. Everywhere structures are failing, whether it is the nation state, organized religion, education, health care, none of our existing institutions can guide us through the transition. They are all structured for separation when what the planet needs is coordination, connectivity, and cocreativity.

This evolutionary shift started I believe, in 1945, when the United States dropped the atomic bombs on Japan. It became obvious that this still self-centered species had gained power to destroy the world, as we know it...or to cocreate a future of immeasurable possibilities. We had gained powers we used to attribute to gods, but we were not wise gods.

In the 60's we began to see the new social patterns emerge which are bearing fruit now and are paving the way for a new world. With Apollo we penetrated our biosphere and saw ourselves as one whole planetary body for the very first time. It was our "birth" on the physical plane as a universal species.

In the same decade the environmental movement arose. We realized that we could destroy our own life support system. That the environment is actually our extended body. And we fell in love with ourselves as a whole.

The great social and consciousness movements developed – peace, civil rights, human rights, and social justice. The "cultural creatives" appeared, the civil society, now growing rapidly like imaginal cells in the body of a caterpillar, resonating with each other, proliferating, about to become a butterfly.

At this same time feminine consciousness was liberated and expressed in millions of us. But something beyond cultural change was happening. It was a bio-evolutionary event. Humanity realized for the first time that we were reaching a population limit on planet Earth. One more doubling of the population would destroy all the children of the world, and much of life itself. The signal went out: Don't be fruitful and multiply up to maximum. Stop!

We began to have chosen children, fewer children, and live longer lives. The passion that had gone into self-reproduction, birthing and nurturing large families expanded into the desire for self-expression, self-evolution, life purpose, and vocation. Self-reproduction was expanding into self-evolution. The miraculous capacity of our bodies to transform to give birth to the child, to nurse, and love that newborn with unconditional love seemed to be extending into the passion to give birth to the authentic feminine self and our expression in the world.

We moved from maximum procreation toward cocreation.

Cocreation is the experience of the creative process of the universe itself localizing in each of us as our unique desire to express and create. It is the God force internalized as our own creativity. This is a power as great as the drive for self-preservation and self-reproduction. It is the desire for self-evolution and the transformation of our world.

But we can't cocreate alone. We want to find others who share our passion to create. "Vocational arousal" awakens. We get excited. We look for others who are excited by us.

A force as great as sex itself awakens. I call it "suprasex." It is the passion to join to cocreate. Not the desire to join our genes to have the babies, but our genius to give birth to our greater selves.

Nature is bringing the pleasure principle into suprasex. We've heard about the Joy of Sex. This is the Joy of Suprasex! It's fun, it's thrilling. We want to do more if it. We can do it many times. But we have to find others who want to join with us to create. Vocational arousal and suprasex are natural forces of creation arising within us. When we do join to cocreate, something new is born in each of us and in the world.

Our creativity is the life force, the divine impulse of evolution rising within us as we hit the limit to population growth on planet Earth.

What's more, as we are having fewer children, chosen children whenever we have the choice, we are also living longer lives. In the past women of my age, (78 and a half) would either be dead, or be grandmothering large families. Now we are here! Millions of us. 50, 60, 70, 80, 90 and counting!

A new phase of life is opening up. I call it Regenopause. It occurs when we find our deeper life purpose and say YES to it. This activates a new vitality, energy and passion within us. We begin to regenerate.

After menopause, when we are no longer producing eggs, we enter the phase of life when we are free to give birth to our full potential self. This process of birthing the feminine self is as profound an act as giving birth to the child. We have not seen this "self" grown up before. There are no models of the fully mature Evolutionary Woman. The world that calls us forth is in fact being cocreated by all of us. We are pioneers. Yet, we are programmed through our hormones for unconditional love of the unknown child. We love that newborn no matter how much of a mess it may be!

This same capacity for unconditional love now applies to birthing and nurturing our essential selves and our expression in the world. Since both the feminine self and the emerging world are unformed, new, often a mess, our love is called into play. We do not have to know what it will be in order to love it. This is motherly evolutionary faith.

My sense is that the millions of women entering Regenopause are embodying a new phase of evolution itself. We are very "young" universal humans, connected through the heart to the whole of life. By young I mean that no one knows how to evolve the person and the world. We are beginners, no matter what age we are. We are in a kindergarten of "godlings." We are new because we are called to give birth to a new type of world, a cocreative world in which each person is free to do and be his or her best. This world has not existed before. And neither have we. Evolutionary Women of all ages, and especially women in Regenopause are almost like a "missing link" in the evolution of our species. We are carriers of the new humanity.

We do not seek to be equal to men in a dysfunctional world, rather to be partners with men and women, cocreative couples and teams giving birth within ourselves to the evolving human and the emerging world. We are joining together spontaneously and naturally, cofounding a new family of humanity.

The Evolutionary Woman is a harbinger of a new world. Whatever age we may be, we are part of one planetary generation. We are facing the new together. No one has been through the transition from a high technology, over-populating, polluting world to a new cocreative world equal to our spiritual, social and scientific/ technological capacity. There are no experts in how to evolve a planet. No one is standing "on the other side" of the transition and telling us what to do.

Who is going to guide us through this jump? It's the intuitive knowing of the larger patterns of creation, the design of evolution, the implicate order unfolding within us and among us that guides us now. The authority is within us. Especially when we resonate with one another in an environment of love and non-judgment. It is right here that Evolutionary Women are birthing each other and our new world.

My latest realization is that we are taking a quantum jump into the present. The time is now and we are here!

Barbara Marx Hubbard
Co-founder of the Foundation for Conscious Evolution
Barbaramarxhubbard.com

Acknowledgements

To the Tuesday night support group who held a space for women to find the courage and inspiration to write; particularly those who held the container: Anne Frances, BB, Billie, Bonnie, Elizabeth, Karen, LaVonne, Marilyn, Pamela, Sage and every woman who joined and gave her gift into the circle.

To Gentle Readers and Editors who gave their love and time to provide reflection and suggestions to the authors. Many of the contributors to the book provided this service to their peers. Others who did not write stories provided this valuable gift also; we'd like to honor them here: Brad Comann, Nina Cooley, Jeanie Derousseau, Connie Eberhart, Jayne Howard Feldman, Julie Heyman, Karen Latvala, Anita Pathik Law, Shelly Rachanow, Elizabeth Stephenson, Michele Wojchiechwokshi, Sharon Ybarra.

To LightPages, our online communication network, that provided a framework for our connection and information sharing during this process. We thank Jeanie Derousseau for developing the system and continuing to evolve it to meet our emerging needs.

We deeply thank Judith Watson who volunteered from the very beginning to do anything we needed. She edited over 35 stories and in the process laughed, cried and transformed from the experience.

ACKNOWLEDGEMENTS

To Christine Kloser, our publisher, and an Evolutionary Woman, who committed to publishing the book as soon as Karen Porter voiced the call that we should write an "Evolutionary Woman's Guide to Life".

And to all the women who have attended our retreats and have cocreated the field of evolutionary resonance from which this book has arisen.

Introduction

LUCKY SWEENY

Evolutionary Women arose out of a community of women and men who had come together to explore the principles and practices of Conscious Evolution. It was Grandmothered by the remarkable and brilliant Barbara Marx Hubbard. And it was birthed by Bonnie Kelley and me on International Women's Day, March 8, 2005.

For several years, Bonnie and I had been meeting in my apartment, which was the second floor of a lovely Victorian house in downtown Santa Barbara. We spent many hours there, talking, meditating, recording our inspirations, listening to angels, planning events and more. It was such a rich time. We were part of founding the Santa Barbara Conscious Evolution Community and served on the Council that coordinated community activities.

Bonnie and I are both Evolutionary Women and we show the diversity of this new feminine archetype. Bonnie is a Christian Scientist, an author, a mother and grandmother, and as she would say the former wife of "three Jewish husbands". Until moving to Santa Barbara, Bonnie had never belonged to anything outside of the PTA and church. Her life was spent in caretaking of her beloved daughter and three husbands, and quietly reading, writing and pursuing her spiritual path. She arrived in Santa Barbara, 5 years divorced, a published author and ready to burst into her magnificence of which she had only a faint inkling.

I, on the other hand, had joined everything I could for as long as I can remember. I had the oddest high school resume. I was captain of the cheerleaders and president of the political club. These were the prefigural archetypes that would manifest in a lifetime dedicated to spiritual development and social activism.

I had my first spiritual awakening experience when I was 20. It was a remarkable experience, brief but permanent. A flash into a larger reality and the clear understanding that THIS is where I am from, a first experience of my origin. Unconscious, really, tripped upon rather then the end of a long steady journey. My understanding was immature and I didn't really know what to make of it. A few days after this event, I stood in my Beacon Street apartment watching the MTA train emerge from the underground just outside my window. And I heard words in my head "Your life will never be the same." And it hasn't been.

Thirty-five years later, Bonnie and I find each other in the "muddy pool" of Conscious Evolution. We shared some childhood conditions, middle class, difficult fathers, and spiritual curiosity from a young age. But as adults we came from different worlds. As unlikely as it seems, we became mirrors for each other and sisters connected at our essence.

As Rumi says:

> Beyond the realms of right and wrong
> There is a field
> I will meet you there

That's where Evolutionary Women are meeting, coming together from our own lives and stories. Looking for what we share in values and practice, in beliefs and commitments, doing our best to experience each other in acceptance, rather then judgment. To see each other as whole beings who are an expression of our essence, which is the individual manifestation of universal reality.

We are human beings, the latest result of 14 billion years of evolution. We are the Big Bang manifesting in the 21st century. This may be a challenging thought. It is true. You know it, because you've read some of the science on this. There was nothing, and then there was everything. The Big Bang created the energy that is now in the atoms of our body. Life, in this solar system, has evolved to us.

As you take hold of this awareness, you will then see yourself in your largest context. You don't have to give up your house, or family, or community or anything. You just have to add that you are the Universe in Person.

You can understand that Universe as a Divine Being, Spirit, Life, Energy. The wonderful thing about evolution is it loves diversity. More choices more opportunities, it's not competition, its cooperation.

We've chosen to work with women because it's what we know. Evolutionary Women has no desire to be separate from men. We work, live and play with and love men, brothers, friends, partners, and husbands. We look forward to creating joint projects with men in the future.

The writers in this book come from all over the U.S. and Canada. They have all attended an Evolutionary Women retreat. The stories are about their lives, families, love, loss, learning, working and being. Each story emerges from the woman's experience as she shares how her choices have influenced her life and expanded her consciousness. There are stories that may bring tears and stories to laugh with.

The process has been dynamically co-creative. As we progressed through the writing, amongst ourselves, we created processes to support each woman to write in a field of acceptance. We practiced the values we have espoused; love, caring, respect and creation.

I thank all the women who have participated; two in particular did truly exceptional work. First, Andrea Hylen served as the project director. She took on the book as a sacred assignment and made every stage of its development a sacred moment. We are all so very grateful to her for her inspired leadership. Andrea is also the newest partner in Evolutionary Women. In 2008, Andrea joined Bonnie and me as a full partner in Evolutionary Women.

The other individual I want to honor is Judith Watson. Judith came to our first East Coast retreat and volunteered to be an editor. With skill and grace, she edited over three-quarters of the stories in the book. Thank you, Judith. I see you as a representative of all the women who partnered with women to complete their writing, who were on the support calls, were "gentle readers," editors and assistants in all aspects of the work.

I've been called Lucky all my life. I got the nickname in the hospital shortly after my birth and it has stuck with me all these years. I'm often asked if I am lucky. I say I am Lucky and it's not an easy name to hold the day after a loved one has died or a relationship ends unexpectedly. But, I have been Lucky to work all my life with some of the greatest women on the planet. Evolutionary Women is the zenith of that experience.

I hope you enjoy the stories. If you're inspired, come be with us at a retreat, send us your thoughts and ideas, and sign up for our newsletter. Mostly, I hope you will find encouragement and support to continue and expand the evolutionary work you are doing where you are. You are the one we've been waiting for.

Lucky Sweeny
May 19, 2008

PART ONE

I Am an
Evolutionary Woman

I Love You Just the Way You Are

ANDREA HYLEN

It was a Friday morning. My two little girls were playing in our living room, Liz rolling around in her seat on wheels while Mary tried to steer and guide her through the massive pile of colorful, wooden blocks already gathering on the rug. I was perched on a chair surrounded by sorted, dirty laundry, eyes glued to the early morning children's programming on TV, waiting for the time in the show where Mister Rogers would tell me that he loved me.

Silently holding my breath, I stared at the TV, waiting for the song.

"It's such a good feeling to know you're alive. It's such a happy feeling you're growing inside."

Why was I in so much pain? My daughters were so beautiful. I was married. We had a sweet little house. I had a job I loved with wonderful, supportive people. What was wrong with me?

"And you'll have things you'll want to talk about. I will, too."

I had ideas I was eager to talk about and explore. I had dreams, hopes, and fears that felt empty inside of me, shriveling into nothingness. Isolated, I felt there was no one who understood. And then

Mister Rogers would say it.

" I love you just the way you are."

The tears silently streamed down my face.

And here it was again, Friday, the day I tried to put some order back into the house after working for four days. It was my day to be home all day loving and mothering my daughters, with my to-do-list in hand. Laundry, grocery shopping, dishes, clean the bathroom, vacuum, sweep and watch Sesame Street and Mister Rogers with my two beloved girls, Mary and Elizabeth.

Every Friday, I grew more exhausted from the conflict that was growing inside of me. Where should I place my attention? What was the priority? Was it more important to read to my daughters or to clean the bathroom? If we took a walk in the park, would I be able to hang the laundry on the clothesline in time for it to dry in the sun? My mind was racing. There was always something left undone.

How did I get here? How did I arrive at the place of feeling so unloved, a place where I didn't know myself, a place where I never seemed to feel good enough?

Searching for answers, I looked back at my own childhood, where I always felt responsible for my mother's emotions. My father traveled with his job during the week, and my mother ran the house. I learned to tune into her ups and downs, the ups and downs we all have in life, thinking her happiness was dependent on me, the good daughter thing.

I grew up at a time when the world was changing for women. We were seeking the same rights, the same pay and the same opportunities as men. Yet, for many women at the time, the desire to be free also seemed to be filled with a lot of anger. Even as a schoolgirl, I wanted to be a part of the freedom, but not the bitterness that seemed to come with it. I both embraced and shunned being female.

I was also growing up in a world where fathers looked at Playboy magazines, and we were told to be on our best behavior when Dad was home. I was told that if I beat a boy at a game, he might not like me. And that was mirrored by the boys who picked me to play on the kickball team because of my home runs, but picked the cute girls cheering on the sideline for a date to the dance.

Through my teen years and into my early twenties, there were times I felt connected to my dreams and desires and to a passion within me. I starred in musicals, twirled show-flags in the marching band in high school and worked for women's health care organizations in college. I felt at home and connected deeply to myself, knowing my purpose. In those moments, I knew who I was and where I was going.

And then I married Bill, a man I met and dated in college. We moved to Baltimore, Maryland, two hours away from our families. Bill began a desk job with the government, as I looked for employment during a recession.

For two months, I had no job, no friends, and no community. I couldn't find employment in social work or in a women's organization. I finally settled for a job as a bank teller, a job I hated and where I felt like an animal caged at the zoo. Still I craved friendships, a sense of community, and something to nourish my soul. Even after I gave birth to our first child and found a job I loved as a research assistant at the University of Maryland, something was missing.

My marriage was falling apart. The only time my husband and I spent together was in the living room with the television turned to the news or the nightly re-runs of MASH. He was content to work on projects in his workshop upstairs with the door closed and the radio turned on. He discouraged me from inviting anyone into the house, and I felt embarrassed that anyone would see how critical he was of me, as well as his drinking.

Hoping church would "solve things," I converted to Catholicism and attended a six-month intensive study program. I read books about family patterns, attended Al-Anon meetings and saw a therapist to explore and understand myself.

I gave birth to our second child. Her arrival was a blessing because I couldn't pretend to have it all together anymore. With little sleep, a job, a house and two kids to take care of, there was nothing left for me.

I was dying inside.

Who was I? I felt so unexpressed and so helpless to receive the attention and love I desired.

My husband's voice became louder in my head than mine. The voices of television, neighbors, parents, and people on the street dominated my thoughts. My inner knowing, my own voice was locked in a closet only to be replaced with "should" expectations: ideas I had created in my mind of what it was to be a valuable, good person.

I was trying to fit into a mold of what I thought life was supposed to look like. I was afraid to create conflict. I struggled to fit into the role of being a "good mother" and "a good wife."

Merging all of the pictures from my childhood and movies and books, I created the image of who I thought I should be. And it almost killed my spirit.

My husband became an incredible mirror of the self-doubt I had inside me. When he criticized my decisions, his outer voice became my inner voice. I had placed so many expectations on myself there was no way I could succeed. I am grateful now that he didn't make it easy for me. He reflected my doubts and fears so loudly, I had to stand up or die!

The path to recovering, reclaiming and finding myself began with listening to my inner voice, even when my family and friends didn't understand my choices. When my choices didn't look like the images around me, I learned to take chances and trust myself. When I saw my little girls watching me, I knew that I was not being the woman, the role-model, I wanted to be for them. An inner strength grew within me and gave me the courage to change.

I left my marriage, found a place to live and continued reading. I learned to balance my needs with raising my children. Painting the walls in my home bright colors and playing music like Patti LaBelle's 'New Attitude' fed my soul. I found ways to become the role model I wanted to be for my daughters, standing up for myself in the court system, leaving an emotionally abusive marriage, and building a community of friends who loved me as I am.

There were signs along the way. I would feel a physical reaction when I felt an internal "no" but said yes. Sometimes it was a sick feeling in my stomach or a prickly feeling that made the hair on my neck stand up. A heart palpitation or achiness was usually an internal shout of NO!

I learned to respond to signs that led me to books, people, community and a deeper connection to my own voice. I began to notice, and I started listening to myself. Writing in my journal and nurturing myself with pink roses and babies breath became an every day part of life.

While writing this story I had a wonderful moment. I was sitting at my computer when I felt a wave of energy flow from within, and tears sprang to my eyes. I felt the presence of Mister Rogers and a rush of gratitude for the gift he gave to me so many years ago. He was a lifeline when I felt so alone. I wondered, was he on television at that moment? Scanning the television guide, I found the channel. YES! There he was sitting in a dentist's chair with his mouth wide open. The dentist was counting his teeth. (Was he telling me to open my mouth and use my voice?)

Later in the show, he sang a song about the gift of a smile. He talked about how wonderful it is to smile, but it is more important to share what you are really feeling. He talked about the importance of letting out the tears, if that is what you are feeling inside. On television, he said he wanted to know how I was really feeling and he told me that he loved me.

Thank you Mister Rogers for loving me when I couldn't love myself. And now, I will take it from here.

Andrea Hylen attended the first Evolutionary Women Retreat in Dec 2005. She listened to her inner Self and studied to become a Minister of Spiritual Peacemaking with the Beloved Community in 2006, to coordinate the first Evolutionary Women Retreat in Baltimore in 2007 and to become the Project Manager for this book. Andrea is also the mother of three amazing Evolutionary Women, Mary, Elizabeth and Hannah and a son, Cooper, now in Spirit. Andrea can be reached at www.AndreaHylen.com

Who Do You Think You Are?

PAMELA MOSLEY

"Young lady, who do you think you are?!"

That question, posed to me by my mother when I was out of line as a child, when I was too bold for her comfort and needed to be pulled back into place, was amazingly effective. For a young lady learning about her place, the tone and implication communicated the great importance of constraint. As I grew, the power and purpose behind the question continued to pull me back to a familiar bounded comfort, and I got used to playing small.

Looking back, I can see how playing small took its toll. Years of denying the parts of my own creative nature that might push the limits of acceptability caused division and dissent within me. Friends would sometimes say that I was hard to get to know. It was my deteriorating physical health that gave me a picture of what was happening. With two abdominal surgeries before age 20 and vascular and bladder spasms starting in my 30s, patterns of the "inner tightness" that I carried came into clearer view. Habits of holding in, holding on and holding back were reflected in my thoughts, feelings and behaviors and had settled into the cells of my body. How I needed to relax!

Then the message that "I am a spiritual being having a human experience" came to me. I remember I read it over and over in a New Age newsletter and cut it out and hung it on my wall. A new way of thinking, and yet strangely resonant at some abandoned place in me. I took an introductory class in body energy work and experienced again both the wild out-of-the-box newness and the oh-yes-I'm-starting-to-remember familiarity of an invisible reality underlying the whole of creation, the whole of me.

Who did I think I was? I remembered that as a young teen I had discovered a poem by June Jordan that so captivated me that I got out construction paper and cut out every letter and re-composed her message, high in my room above the curtains. It was:

I am
impossible to explain
remote from old and new interpretations
and yet
not exactly

There was boldness in posting these assertions of my very essence. The aliveness that they stirred in me was persistent and inviting. Alongside the ingrained habits that I had acquired of saying "no" to any out-of-bounds impulse, there was also an enduring pull to a deeper "yes."

Following that pull began to rearrange my life. With additional energy classes, I began to perceive the subtle vibrational language of life and marveled at the new world opening up to me. What amazing multidimensional beings we are! How whole-making to acknowledge the truth of it! How refreshing to reclaim Spirit's vibrant presence! It seemed that a world nearly lost to me had been brought back from the dim edges of my awareness and was being revived as my expanding experience of reality.

My awakening to this larger context activated a response in me like a quickening. I felt the dormant parts of me rising and wanting to live. "There is more of me," I kept thinking. Who did I think I was? Without consciously planning it, I noticed I was using my full name more often. It helped to reflect the expanding sensation of self I was experiencing. It seemed that opening to the fullness of my being had set a particular process into motion. As I continued to say, "yes" to this unfolding process, I came up against the hard "rules" of thought and conduct so well established in me. Yet I could taste the new freedom and potential wanting to be born. I described it like this:

The closer I get
to the Center of me
the more I approach Truth.
And I cry.

Coming nearer to the core of me was like opting for a meltdown. I felt an inevitable attraction to draw near the fire even while the heat was burning off armor that felt like flesh. I had reached a point of choice: either I could choke off the life force from moving too much in me, numbing myself and going through the expected motions of living or, By God, I could give myself as fully as I knew how to what had been calling me by name and freely enter in to the passion of Life. The tears came as my restraint softened.

Letting down my guard has been a gradual process. At first I re-member waves of panic. It seemed it was the restrictions that had been holding me together and defining me. Who would I be if I let them all go? What would be left? Was this even a good idea?

Again, my body provided the guidance forward. At times it felt very fragile. I learned to give it regular times of rest and silence and solitude. I respected its messages. And I gave it permission to dance. When the longing to let out overcame the practice of holding in, the body knew the movements it needed to unwind and express. It is through my body that I most commune with the Center of me. In motion and in stillness, it is through the substance of the body that the union of spirit and form is known to me. In that communion, restrictions fall away. And there rises a knowing that that communion is who I am.

I've come to see that letting go of restrictions is my greatest gift to myself and to the world. I feel how this conflicts with pressures in and around me to stay small and bound for comfort's sake. Yet, in giving in to those pressures, I turn from my true identity, and my experience of life is diminished. As I relate and respond to that which is highest within me, I'm led forward in new and unpredictable ways that invite me to grow into more of who I am. Again and again, I return to Center and allow a process of sacred molting as each layer of false belief comes up to be seen and released.

I feel lighter now than ever before. I've come to know a peace that resonates throughout my being as a pleasurable ease. This buoyant tranquility remains with me when I am absorbed in the uplifting pull of Center. It is so unlike my old pattern of "keeping the peace," which was constricting to me and others. And the more I continue to relax into my larger Presence, the more I know myself to be a part of an ongoing process of creative intent. It is as if Life itself lives through me, moving through whatever has been yielded, to bring about liberation and emergence on an ever-larger scale.

When I am intentionally together with others responding to this same Life pulse in them, the intrinsically uplifting momentum is intensified. I love to consider the magic that will be invoked when we release all our props and relax completely into the presence of Center! I imagine it like this:

I AM
in the quiet
stillness of my being
aware of a vast unbounded utter greatness
that opens still wider when **2 or 3** are gathered in that place
a transcendent
lively awakening **critical** to summoning all
toward home where thunderous light of
unmatched **mass** activates a
flooding cataclysm of Joy
and cellular revolutions cascade in universal pulsations of
response
coming to settle in a higher plateau of being because
aware of a vast unbounded utter greatness
in the quiet stillness
of my being
I AM

I know myself to be a portal for the most powerful energy in the Universe to move through. I know myself to be that energy! No longer can I identify myself with a nature which is not divine. Divine Presence is what remains as my resistance is released. A process of restoration is underway in me whereby body, mind and heart awaken to Oneness with the abiding Presence. This seems to be in process for us all.

What deep appreciation I feel for this most fundamental question: Who do you think you are?

Pamela Mosley's *favorite mantra is "Let Love Radiate." As an Attunement Practitioner, her joy is in connecting with others in that shared sacred space and opening to the radiant presence of Love for personal and planetary transformation. She lives and moves and has her being among a lively awakening community in Conway, Arkansas. Contact her at (501)450-9097 and visit www.truetothelightwithin.com or www.fcssc.org*

She invites you to R.S.V.P. . . . Reclaim Spirit's Vibrant Presence!

Removing the Mask

BB HARDING

This story is about someone who spent a lifetime hiding.

It isn't that I chose to go into hiding; it is much more that it was easier to withhold my voice than make waves. The result left me in the wake of indecision, procrastination, full of fear and riddled with self-doubt. There are many who would look at me and would never perceive these things about me. Many are buoyed by my courage, the wisdom that I hold, the outrageousness of expression; and yet, I know that I am less than I could be. One might hold that I have high expectations of myself, and that would be true. How can I convey that from a multi-dimensional perspective, I know that I am all powerful, and yet I can not even ease my own pain; that I am all-knowing, and yet I can not determine the best course of action for my life; that I am a creator and yet, I can not seem to manifest any one of my heart's desires. This sense of unease has plagued me for most of my life – the knowing on one level, and the inability to execute on another. How could such a wimpy being be a reflection of the Goddess in all her power and beauty?

As I get older I find that the energy of my thoughts tend to get coagulated around what I can't do. A lifetime of can do is becoming a life filled with can'ts. I can't control myself; I can't undertake that activity – too strenuous; I can't do that, it will take too long. There is a sense of morbidity that foments throughout my life. I seem to be plagued with one word that defines me: "mediocre." Someone who is operating at less than full capacity; someone willing to settle rather than be totally integrous with her inner self; someone who accepts excuses rather than take radical personal responsibility; and someone who has closed her eyes rather than come fully awake. The wake up gong has sounded, and it clearly says that I need to choose to live. Choose to undertake those things that would support me in living a wholesome life; choose to strive for something great even if I don't believe it possible; choose to BE who I am. The first thought that I have is how can I possibly BE who I am when I have no idea of what that might be? I am always saying I don't know what I want to be when I grow up. And in that dilemma comes the lack of decision to choose to grow up. A friend of mine recently told me that I no longer get to bitch about not knowing who I am and my purpose in life – for deep down I know. If it is absolutely necessary to gripe, then gripe about how hard it is to be here on planet earth, but not about not knowing why I am here.

That few moments of wisdom have turned me into someone frantically trying to define who I am. I have spent years exploring, years trying on new things, years praying to be granted an understanding as to what my unique gifts are, years yearning for something that gives my life meaning and purpose. Things attract me like so much glitter, and get thrown away after the party is over. There are bits and pieces that come together, but nothing seems grand enough to be the being that I desire to be. Therein lies a key to the dilemma – how desire does not match reality, and then the gulf becomes undoable. It proves difficult to be humble and able to simply accept what is and then from that place allow the creation to move forward. Even on this project, a collaborative effort of evolutionary women sharing their stories, I have secretly wanted to participate, yet completely withheld my desire to do so. If I am honest, I see that I really want to play with others, yet I hover at the outskirts of the circle, afraid to ask for inclusion for fear that I will be rejected. The voiceover is strong – I have too much to do to take time to write this; I have nothing to say in comparison to what others do (after all, I am not a powerful political leader; I do not own a business, I am not a mover and shaker in any world; I have little influence in any particular area) and hell, I still strongly doubt that I AM an Evolutionary Woman.

As I dig below, I find that many of the "I can't possibly do that's" come from a place that holds the picture of perfection that is so "not real" for me. My first thoughts of an evolutionary woman are that she is someone who is so clear about what she wants to accomplish that she is able to control her destiny; she walks into the room and everyone turns their head to see who she is; she is someone who speaks, and everyone listens to what she says. In short, she walks on water and easily creates miracles. A far cry from the being that I perceive myself to be, i.e., someone who has hidden in the shadows for much of her life and could never in a million years do that – be that – or have that.

The place that I fear to go most of all is inside. How can there possibly be anything inside worth loving? I have looked outside for so long and know the shortcomings of that being. Am I willing to go within and discover--even love--the beauty of that which lives inside? So what does she have to say about what an evolutionary woman is? Several weeks ago, I did sit down to write about what is an evolutionary woman? The response:

> An evolutionary woman has her heart tuned to the Mother. She allows her feelings to be evident and strives to be a pure reflection of love. She acknowledges her multi-dimensional-

ity. She acts as guide and mentor to the children, those that are lost, those that are seeking. She places herself in the mainstream of every-day reality and converts the disharmonious energies into peace, tranquility and love. She is adventuresome – meaning that she is aligned to living the mysteries of the soul; she is dedicated to finding the purest of expressions; she is nurturing, a safe haven for all passers-by; and among all things loves her own essence. She seeks to see the greater picture of evolution and guides mankind on that journey. She is a synthesizer of knowledge – past, present and future. She gathers to herself the nurturance and support and those who share her vision. She is an illuminator, a visionary, a beacon, a soul experiencing the pleasures of 3D. She is open to infinite possibilities and creates her dreams into reality.

Ok, so I am not all of these things, and I am some of these things. Some parts of this are quite lofty, some parts exhilarating; some I can connect with, and some create shaky knees. And because it comes from me, I have to acknowledge that my soul knows that all of this is possible, and more importantly, it is possible for me. In the effort (and trust me, at this time I do mean effort) to be a fuller expression of myself, I find that I am willing to allow myself to be rebirthed once again this year. I find that the willingness to love that, which is, begins to grant me the compassion to forgive myself for all my transgressions. That finally, out of the shadows, is someone who is rising to the occasion; someone willing to take another risk; someone willing to find a new way of living and sharing; someone who is willing to be vulnerable; someone who is willing to be supported by others; someone who is willing to guide and lead on a conscious level. The desire to lead has been accompanied with the fear to lead. For in leading there is a form of responsibility that I have never really wanted to have (after all, I could be leading others down the wrong path). At the same time,

I am consciously willing to lay an energetic trail for others to ride. Perhaps it will serve as an inspiration for one other person to choose to live again. For at this time, I choose once again to reach for a star, no matter how far away it may be. I am willing to acknowledge that I AM AN EVOLUTIONARY WOMAN, even though I know not where that leads.

BB Harding is an eclectic individual. She currently works as an IT project manager; has written a book called Essential Oil Wisdom that will be published in the summer of 2008; and has a passion for whales, especially the humpbacks. As a member of the Messenger Network, she is exploring the possibilities of providing a space for young messengers to display how they are making a difference in the world.

Choosing An Open Heart

KAREN PORTER

As a young boy, my Dad carried his older brother after rheumatic fever weakened the brother's heart. When his first grandchild was diagnosed as hydrocephalic and my brother was told that his daughter might never walk, my father's reaction was, "If we have to carry her for the rest of her life, we will. You do what you have to do."

That was my Dad's mantra: You do what you have to do.

With this model of determination, I have in my varied careers seen need and filled it. As a small business owner, I organized the first neighborhood business association map in Baltimore City. As a crisis worker, I started support groups for the parents of sexually abused children and led mothers' groups while children were in therapy for witnessing domestic violence.

I was the first parent to travel to the Soviet Union to adopt a child. Seeing the conditions in my younger son's orphanage, I began sending back medicine, toys, and clothing. Partnering with another adoptive mom, we founded Children in Common to support adoptive families and the orphanages that were their children's first homes. When we learned the fate of the kids when they "age out" of the orphanage system, we funded training programs so they would have marketable skills and independent living experience to be prepared for life when they leave institutional care.

Recognizing that kids coming from institutions had many delays and issues children adopted from foster care did not have, I networked with families who had adopted kids from Romania (Romania opened to international adoption a year before the USSR) and learned all I could about post-institutionalization. When my friend, the co-founder of CIC, started an international program for a local adoption agency, I developed a training program for adopting couples to prepare them for the challenges of parenting a post-institutional child.

When my developmentally delayed sons were not ready for the academic stresses they faced within the school system, we home schooled them for eight years.

When my mother, after a two-year process of surgery, chemotherapy, and radiation, needed help to finish all the things she wanted to do before she left this life, I was there. I helped her make lists of what she wanted to give to whom, label items, and go through photo albums her mother had assembled. I assured her that I would carry out her wishes, deliver the letters she wrote to each family member, and take care of my Dad. I was one of her caretakers at the end of her life. I was with her when she took her final breath.

All these choices were good deeds; good work, benefiting countless people. Yet I did all these things with a closed heart. I had learned to protect myself, to make myself impenetrable and safe from hurt because I knew what it was to be hurt.

Sexually abused by an uncle-in-law from the age of three, I was used and raped for eight years until he saw that I was beginning my first period. That final rape was particularly brutal. I thought I was dying. I hurt. I bled. Not knowing anything about the abuse, my mother told me about periods and the body preparing to have babies. I shut down. Part of me believed that a demon baby waited inside me.

It was only a matter of time before it would begin to grow.

My psychological pain manifested in physical pain. My periods were debilitating. No number of tampons or pads kept the flow from staining my underpants and running down my legs.

That uncle died when I was in my early twenties. Fortunately, incest survivors' therapy was starting then. I found a therapist who gave me back my life. I began to date and met the man who would become my husband. David is a sweet guy and part of me knew I would be safe with him. The more dominant part of me trusted no one.

Trusting few people very little, I lived my life. Through work, school, miscarriages, adoption, helping families here as well as children on the other side of the globe, I let no one in. I spent time with people, shared knowledge, and supported others, but I did not let them know me. I did a good job always and managed to guard my heart along the way, never sharing myself, never risking hurt.

The women I met in the home school community were amazing. Home school moms are super mama-bears, going against the establishment, withstanding pressure and criticism to do what each thinks is best for her child. So along with likeminded, fierce, firebrand moms, I attended meetings and joined book groups. I grew in spirit in the company of women. I trusted them a bit more than I had been willing to trust anyone before.

We moved, the boys entered a small private school, and I lost touch with all but a couple of the home school moms. Then, a year ago, I had the chance to reconnect. They had joined forces to bring an Evolutionary Women retreat to Baltimore. The possibility of rejoining this vibrant group of women was exciting. Could I take the risk? Could I tell them how much I missed being part of their community? I feared I would be judged for having my sons re-enter the school system. The last book group I had been in with them had ended badly, and I was afraid that old wounds and unresolved issues would surface.

That retreat was life altering. While the attendees were all ages and had different jobs and life experiences, we shared a commitment to support other women and be supported in self-actualizing. We honored our inner wisdom and individual gifts and as we joined together, our combined respect and shared intentions created an atmosphere of safety that allowed me, for the first time in my life, to speak from my heart with little fear. As the weekend was ending, I shared with the group that my heart had opened and what I feared was going back into a world without safe places and opportunities to share at such a deep level.

After the retreat, two of the moms with whom I reconnected began an "Art of Spiritual Peacemaking" book group. I knew the author, James Twyman, his music and his message of peacemaking. James founded The Beloved Community, and I had taken several of his online classes. These two women had become ministers and seminary facilitators for The Beloved Community. This new group became my safe haven. Going through the book, I again opened my heart. The lessons in the book became lessons for my life. I felt joy. I accepted myself, saw the perfection in everything I had experienced, and was grateful for everything in my life. Every situation had its gift, and all my life experiences had helped form me. To further my own evolution, I entered and completed the seminary program, cracking open further at the Beloved Community retreat where I was ordained a Minister of Spiritual Peacemaking.

Within the teachings of the seminary program, one of the processes was a walk of forgiveness where you forgive others and yourself. I forgave many people on many levels, and when it was time to walk the forgiveness of my ultimate abuser, I did. The primal sounds that came from deep within me both frightened me and freed me. I sobbed the words, and I was supported by a fellow seminarian, one of the home school moms, the one with whom I had the falling out years before. I was blessed with many levels of healing.

I continue to struggle to keep my heart open. I do not want to return to living a self-protective life with a closed heart. Out of the seminary program and Evolutionary Women retreats, a group of us home school moms and a few others have formed an ever-evolving group we named "The Peace Sisters." We meet weekly to support each other, to deepen our individual growth, and build community. We consciously relate from a deep level of openness and honesty and work towards shared goals. As we continue to meet, we share on profound levels, witness each other's struggles and growth. We are bringing our gifts to the world and work to empower others through activities, workshops, and events. As we change our relationships and our ways of relating, as we learn new ways of being and growing together that are not focused on our kids or projects, it is a struggle to keep my heart open, to not fall into old patterns of reacting and distancing.

This year, David and I will be married for twenty-four years. This past Valentine's Day, I gave him a card I made at a Peace Sisters' gathering. In it, I wrote that I loved him and that I was beginning to trust his love for me. I am choosing to trust. I am making the choice to stay open, to share, and to be guided by my heart, to love and feel loved. Each time I consciously choose to stay open, I am scared. This is still very new territory for me. It is uncomfortable. I will tolerate the fear because I want the joy.

When I look back on what I have chosen to do in my life, I see good things. I may have done them with a closed heart--a guarded heart--and they are still good. What I did helped many people. Mother Theresa said that no one can do great things, but we can do small things with great love. I think the difference in choosing to act with an open heart, sharing parts of myself I had not felt safe to do before now, is that the good that is done is good for me as well as others. By opening my heart, I can now receive. I believe what my dad said, that you do what you have to do.

Now I know what I have to do is keep living with an open heart. By doing this, I live in joy.

Karen Porter, *husband David, three cats, and two sons (when they are home from college) live in Towson, MD. Karen co-founded Children in Common (www.childrenincommon.org), to provide relief for children remaining in orphanage care. Karen was named "Knitter of the Year" for 2007-08 by Knitter's Magazine. Karen is a Minister of Spiritual Peacemaking and Seminary Facilitator for the Beloved Community (www.emissaryoflight.org) and Peace Sister (www.thepeacesisters.org). Write Karen at kdstrack@comcast.net*

To Be of Consequence

JEANIE DeROUSSEAU

When I was just 6 years old, my grandparents carried me off to my first day of school. They lived on the same Wisconsin farm where I grew up, so it was easy for them to pick me up and drive the 5 miles to St. Joseph's Elementary School in town.

I sat in the back seat of their grey Packard by myself, waiting for what would happen, feeling on the verge of something important, but small and enveloped by upholstery that stretched in all directions. I could barely see Mimier and Pipier in the front seat, and they didn't talk at all.

We were late, so my class had already walked over to attend Mass. Mimier walked me to the church door, shushed me inside, and left.

The church was brown with shadows, an immense space with hushed smells and expectations. It was just like the car... much too big for me, and I was so small, and no one was seeing me. I don't know how long I stood there crying, but eventually a nun came and walked with me to an appropriate pew. The feeling of being left completely alone to face something much too big for me returns to tempt me to this day.

* * *

When I was fourteen years old, Pipier had a stroke. It was decided that he would stay at home, and that I would sleep with Mimier in case something happened during the night. As I lay on my feather tick mattress waiting for Mimier to come upstairs, I could hear Pipier's labored breathing in the opposite room. Then came a moment I still hear whenever I think about it. I heard three intakes of breath, very raspy and long, and then not another sound.

I got out of bed to look into Pipier's room, and I couldn't see his belly moving. So I called to Mimier from the top of the stairs, afraid to leave his side entirely, and afraid to stay. The aloneness was unbearable. When she came, a minute or an hour later, I held my breath as she shook his shoulder. Yet, some part of me knew very well that he had died.

Mimier didn't register any of the feeling I was having, that something extraordinary had happened. She asked me to pray, briefly kneeling at Pipier's side with me, and then told me to stay with him and continue praying, while she went to telephone my dad and her other children.

I don't know how long I knelt there. I don't remember when my dad or the other relatives came, or when I left Pipier's side. My next memory is of my Dad looking at me in the kitchen, saying, "Go home, Carol Jean." As I ran across the dark field to my own house, I was sobbing. I was six years old again, facing the unknown, without Mimier noticing that I had feelings at all.

* * *

These moments are the most dramatic of a growing up filled with my own inconsequence. My mother was a fifties housewife, my father, a dairy farmer. The farm we lived on with my grandparents was filled with pigs, chickens, horses and cows when I was very young, but soon specialized into cows, and more cows. And Mimier was the matriarch.

There were countless decisions Mimier made on the farm that impacted my life. When my parents were ready for a home of their own, she had a house moved from a neighboring farm she purchased, and it became our home. She decided that we didn't really need a bathroom. So for all my growing up years, our family of 7 made do with a sink in the kitchen, a toilet stool in the basement, and an outdoor toilet. (We went over to her house on Saturday nights to take a bath in her second bathroom.)

Mimier was also a prominent member of the Catholic parish where I went to school. She attended Mass almost every day, and when it was cold enough, she would wear her mink coat. The quality of that coat stays with me. Mimier, rich and luxuriant, soft and beautiful, attending Mass, being a good woman. It is matched by another picture... of Mimier opening her little black coin purse, not very far, peering closely to find just the right coin. I could only touch with longing her mink coat of affection for me, because all I really received was the jealously guarded pennies.

Gradually over the years, I came to understand the many lessons that my grandmother's example taught me: they had to do with power, money, the Catholic Church, love, but at the deepest level, Mimier taught me that my experience was of no consequence. I felt myself rejecting her in return, rejecting power, money, the Church, to protect myself from this deepest wound... that my very being was of no significance to her.

* * *

I woke one morning early in the process of conceiving this chapter, remembering a great achievement of my eighth year. I had finished reading Treasure Island by myself and for myself. No one told me to do it; no one suggested it. I just decided to do it, and I did! And when I finished, I was so proud to have mastered such big words and unfamiliar dialects. But no one recognized my great achievement…

For as long as I can remember, I've been nursing a wound about this failure of my family to support and honor me, to see me and what I had done. And now as I woke that morning, I myself recognized what I had really done. I had experienced an inner impulse to challenge and grow myself. I empowered myself to step forward into action, valuing that impulse enough to read the whole book!

As I stayed with this new understanding, I could feel associations inside of me begin to shift. First I realized that my mother, the house-wife, with little in the way of personal accomplishments, had probably modeled this route of self-empowerment for me. She read whenever she could. Then I began to re-consider my grandmother.

Shortly after that realization, I was in a circle of women being asked to share the name of one woman who has inspired me, and why (for International Women's Day). I felt my face flush as I realized that it was my grandmother, my Mimier, who was coming to mind. In one of those moments when the world changes, I began to see her from another perspective, not as the child ignored, but as the woman I've become, who can empathize and understand.

When I spoke to the circle about Mimier, I said, "My grandmother had seven children, and five miscarriages. She was a victim of the de-pression and told us many times about having to cut up her wedding gown to make undergarments for her girls. She raised her family in a small building with three rooms, and worked on the farm as well. And when she could, she insisted on buying a mink coat and a bathroom for herself. She valued her own experience in an era and culture that didn't do it for her. It was undoubtedly difficult for her to do so, and she may not have been particularly graceful, but she did it."

As I spoke, I knew the truth of this for Mimier. She gave herself "importance." The same way I read my book because I decided to do it, she empowered herself to act in her own interests. I don't know the full reality of her life, what she was like under the pressures of the depression, how selfless she was, but it may be that she, too, found it difficult to value her own experience. It may be that the flow of giving to those who depended on her was so inexorable that at some point she chose to shut herself down emotionally, to become less sympathetic to others, so that she could flow something back to herself.

Not understanding the complexity of her life from my child-centric viewpoint, I constructed a different explanation for why she was the way she was. And it was all about me; I made myself the reason; I made the wrongness something wrong with me. And it colored my entire life…

* * *

The process of reviewing these early life set-points together with other women engaged in the same process has been extraordinary. So much understanding has flowed, changing my past, informing my present, that I have been hard pressed not to revise and revise. I find I must add one new understanding about my grandmother that has been very significant for me…

After Pipier died, it was decided that I would stay with Mimier over the winter to ease her transition. I had no say in the matter. Day after day, month after month during my 14th year, I would walk over to Mimier's house and sleep in the same bed with my grandmother, who would then feed me breakfast in the morning. I gained 20 pounds that winter, and a deep resignation to a life direction of responsibility and inconsequence.

Two memories stay with me from that time… I remember Mimier showing me how she could pull a bobby pin through her pierced ear, and another time, opening the cross over her bed, and laying out for me the ritual items it contained for giving Last Sacraments to a dying person. I can still feel the semi-darkness surrounding me, the hushed voice of my grandmother. For years these memories have been slightly horrific to me, or at the very least, confusing.

I woke last week to an incredible new understanding... that my grandmother had been sharing with me something significant to her, something deeply personal. With awe I could see that she had been actually relating to me as a person... as someone with whom she could share her secrets, as someone of consequence to her.

Jeanie DeRousseau. I am a child of the sixties, entering my sixties. My professional life included: BA, University of Chicago, 1965; MA and PhD Northwestern University, 1973, 1978; tenured position as Associate Professor, New York University, 1986; approximately 50 publications in Physical Anthropology. I am currently a "participant-observer" of the personal/global experience of humankind evolving. I practice resonant evolution on two Councils, with the Santa Barbara Conscious Evolution community and Gather the Women Global Matrix, and with my husband Jeff Eisen and daughter Ariel. With Bruce Schuman, I'm co-evolving LightPages (www.LightPages.net), a self-organizing "online gathering place offering people and their organizations a unique opportunity to come together in resonance in deep partnership with Evolutionary Women." [derousseau@aol.com or 805-637-4671]

Mastering our Feminine/Masculine: Stepping Into Divine Balance

LORI ANN DAVID

"There is no use trying," said Alice; "One can't believe impossible things."
"I dare say you haven't had much practice," said the Queen. "When I
was your age, I always did it for half an hour a day. Why, sometimes I've
believed as many as six impossible things before breakfast."
-LEWIS CARROLL

My earliest memories are of being one with nature. This wonderful presence I was able to claim at a young age gave me the strange distinction of being nicknamed "the happening" by my siblings and the neighbor kids. This "going off alone into nature thing" disturbed most everyone close to me, save my grandfather, who taught me to hunt, fish and all other things deemed to be "for boys."

I was raised to be self-reliant and strong; taught to fix mechanical things, make needed or desired things with tools, whether a sewing machine and fabric or a saw and wood, or growing food and making meals to share. I have a distinct memory of there being no separation of worlds, that it was OK to be a girl yet spend all day in a boat on the wild, wide ocean looking for fish or tramping all day with Gramps, the dogs and guns, looking for deer, yet ending up with pheasant. Or ripping seams for my grandmother and making my own clothes for years. No one said, "This is for boys, and that is for girls"-yet it was quietly heard in the unspoken that I would somehow "grow out of it all." I believe we all start out in feminine/masculine balance inside, in our souls, and we are so pulled by external demands, we lose it and spend most of our lives reclaiming it!

I became increasingly aware of the two worlds-one of maleness, and male things and one of femaleness and female things as I came into my teens and young womanhood. I had many desires and diverse abilities that were clearly pieces of my wholeness. This intensified with the agony between my parents. My heart was ripped wide open, with nothing ahead of me but choices, in very different, unclear worlds. Who were these women and men so dramatically affecting my life? Everything was so confused; who was supposed to be doing what? I had, up until that point, many fine examples of strength, commitment, protection, logic, financial stability, home stability, nurturing, caring, love, peace, some seeming administered, stewarded, learned and given by women, and others by men...

A SHIFT.....

My parent's divorce forced a new reality and something unfolded in me like a big roll of fabric, unwinding down a steep hill. Going to nature soothed my aching mind and fractured spirit. It was clear to me that I was going to have to be whole-strong, assert my will and voice, yet be tender and loving to myself and those around me who were suddenly missing pieces of themselves. I, an individual, had to be responsible for my self in all ways--financially, emotionally, anything that was necessary to live a whole life. I had to use all my energy-energy of words, thoughts, actions-all births, things coming into being in a new way for everyone around me, including myself. I had to muster confidence I never had before. It was almost too much rich wisdom. I knew that the masculine and feminine resided in each of us, and it would manifest differently inside to ourselves, and outside to the world, but that to be completely and spiritually whole, there had to be a balance, outside gender, outside expected roles, outside of a norm that had been carved almost in stone that did not work.

We can't physically be both men and women simultaneously, but spiritually we can have both masculine and feminine energy, which, used in balance, is invincible. All alone toward sunset, near the creek, I realized we are all the same-divine blended beings of universal truths, based in equality of masculine and feminine and right action based on personal integrity. I knew then and there that for whatever reason I would do and be every and any thing I wanted to be in life with no fear, no reservation, no regret. Just love. I was humbled by this precious gift that swirled inside me! I was surrounded by a broken world divided into he's and she's and false roles with unspoken expectations laced in serious blame, disappointment, and truly, ruin. "She" was supposed to do this because she was a woman; "he" was supposed to that because he was a man. She really shouldn't do that because she is blah-blah-blah--enough!

BALANCE

This began my life-long quest to truly understanding the divine feminine/divine masculine, and how to balance them in each of us to be the most incredible individual we can each be. I studied the scientists' approach to reproduction and protection, the analysts' and psychologists' perspective on behavioral traits of men and women, who has what and what crosses over and how we each act and react--on and on....and the historians' perspectives of war and domination, power over and against as opposed to power with and in collaboration/co-creation, the new spiritual therapists' view on the male physical/spiritual side of the body vs. the same for the female side, the energy channels and hormones, indigenous cultures' contribution in tradition and practicality...and more. Within this, lies my message.

HEART

It all comes down to the heart. While there is much debate about masculine/feminine balance, the place it occurs is in our core, in the heart. We all feel, we all love, we all have compassion; we all have power and tenacity, to lead and to follow, to co-create, to be vulnerable, to be objective-all aspects that have been divided into" these are male" and "these are female"-but the truth is they all reside in each of us! Somewhere along the line, for all sorts of reasons, valid and invalid, we split girls over here, boys over there. The gap in our feminine physical/spirit and masculine physical/spirit widened over time in different ways, and with different cultures and societies. We are currently surrounded at this point in time/history with the masculine "eclipsing" the feminine. Such a powerful image-the masculine "obscuring" the "light" of the feminine; surpassing the importance. Oh! Remember this? The hero never ultimately reaches his goal without the assistance of the heroine -female and male balance, always, coming from within! There may be an outside catalyst, muse, event of some soul shaking magnitude, but it goes straight to our core-the heart- and therein lies the change-

I realized that if I did not make choices and decisions from my heart, it did not feel good. Intuition was a huge voice in my being; it took me a long time to get quiet enough to listen to it. The only correct personal path for each of us in life is right action, which comes from listening for and then speaking the truth and taking responsibility for our actions in the world. Being strong and being soft. Being aggressive with knowledge, not necessarily power. It is hard work to open the heart with acceptance and detachment to attain an energy you can feel as strong, soft, and subtle power in the form of pure light. Creative and analytical. In order to be good for anyone else, you need to be good for yourself. It's an ongoing relationship-a conscious commitment to your self to integrate the energies of the heart, mind, and body. And it all comes easier if it is done from a place of passion and playfulness. When this happens for an individual, it is inspiring to others and allows us to be present, not only for ourselves, but them as well. To integrate our own unique divine path empowers others to step into their balance-the ultimate internal balance in an individual of masculinity and femininity, on multiple levels and ways of being, while retaining your true essence/self, whether you are a woman or a man-The divine balance!

TAKE A STEP

Here is what I have heard- "How have you become who you are, or how have you accomplished all these diverse things in your life? What was your motivation? How can one person do and be all of who you are? Where does this energy come from to inspire others?" It has taken me years to respond in a way that truly answers the questions. These "integrations" may seem simple, but here is what I know- how I believe I came into my divine balance.

Fear has no place in life, unless there's a real life threatening event. It is probably the single most fact that we paralyze ourselves with-and many of our reasons are not valid-but shields we have learned to hold up-that keep us from our own divine evolution toward this "balance". There are many ways to "step through this shroud".

Death, or divine completion, is inevitable. We are born, constantly changing, with a shelf life-and there is a powerful force to make the most of our journey-Love-and especially, love the life you wake up to every day, no matter what it is. Be in open-hearted gratitude for whatever crosses your path-and sometimes, that is very difficult to do-There is a gift and message in every moment.

Truth is so powerful and complete. Once we learn to be completely honest with ourselves, from our hearts, we will want to be no other way, no matter what, with ourselves and others. Life is so rich on its own, that the truth is so much more wild and wonderful than anything else, like lying; editing, withholding, and concealing-there are so many names and ways for this "other way", yet ultimately, truth prevails.

Blame has no place in language or action. Be responsible for yourself in every way and moment.

Love is in us and around us at every moment when we choose from the heart with gratitude.

Living in right action from our hearts inspires and motivates others and creates a personal energy of empowerment.

Approaching anything in life with passion from your deep core with an attitude of playfulness creates ease, joy, and abundant living.

Lori Ann David, *"Renaissance Woman" is an inspirational muse. Former competitive athlete/scientist, she lives as farmer/adventurer/artist/healer. Landscape ArtDesign, her design/build firm of 28 years, merges with Sacred Space, a private retreat facility within her sustainable living environment, Casa De Los Angelitos/Aurora Farms. Mother of teens, an active coach for Women in Business, she maintains her life-long passion in aviation as a pilot and educator.*

E-mail loriann@landscapeartdesign.com for the free inspirational newsletter from Sacred Space.

Diversity

CARA MICHELE NETHER

Dear Friend,

Diversity has been one of the most crucial factors in our planetary evolution and human survival. Because of the diversity among humans on our planet, we have been able to create wonders never imagined. In a universal sense, you, with all your uniqueness, are an integral part of the bigger evolutionary plan.

I love the phrase, "Not all who wander are lost." If I needed to sum up my life's journey, that is what I'd most likely say. Short of a few trips to Canada, I have never been further west than Minnesota or further north than New York State. I've covered more ground experientially than geographically during the first forty years of my unconventional life.

Sometime in my late twenties I realized that being a black, gay woman qualified me to be a "triple minority." Identifying as black, gay and female has filled my life with many complications and oppressions that often come with being different. When my family moved from Washington, DC to rural Maryland, the all white neighborhood we settled in gave me my very first experiences of racism. Even though our harassment was minor, this was enough to send a message to me that I was different, and that some people didn't think that was okay.

In my early teens, I realized that I was different because of my attraction to other girls. Even though my family was very open and encouraged me to talk about things that were going on in my life, it was clear to me that I couldn't tell them about these feelings. When my parents found out about my sexual orientation, my entire family was shaken to its core and my life was forever altered. I spent the better part of twenty years condemning myself, trying to change, wanting and attempting to die, and constantly apologizing. I found myself in a schizophrenic dance, going back and forth between trying to find meaning and understanding in my pull toward women, but believing that I must be wrong because of the pain I had caused my family. My family's inability to understand and embrace me wholly was extremely painful to me and created a chasm between us that would not begin to heal for many years. As a result, I felt alone and separated from the people I trusted the most.

On the issue of femaleness, I've slowly come to understand the challenges of being a woman in a male driven society. As I think back on some of the more oppressive and hurtful lessons of being female, ironically, most of them came from other women. "It's important to find a good man who can take care of you," was an important spoken and unspoken mantra for the women around me. This statement made it clear that being a man was held in higher regard than being a woman. Even though women talked about being self sufficient and independent, I observed a mentality and sensed an underlying belief that women really couldn't get what they wanted and needed for themselves. They had to procure a man who could get it for them. A raw sense of survival came into play that produced mistrust among these women, though it was rarely spoken. And there seemed to be only one real way to be a woman. Because I showed very little interest in wearing dresses, high heels, and makeup, or being pretty according to our society's standards, I was told that I would never be a woman. That was devastating news coming from the women I idolized.

To add to the diversity in my life, I had more than ten different jobs and careers before the age of thirty. My formal work experience started at age fifteen. I got my first job working as a counselor at local summer camp. From there I went on to work in the fast food industry; service counter jobs on my college campus; three or four years as a volleyball referee; several years as a picture framer; about ten years as a textile screen printer; two or three years as a house manager for mentally handicapped adults; and several years as a crisis counselor. Later, I worked as a playground safety inspector, carpenter, and owner of a company that designed, built and maintained playground equipment. I also worked as a patient transporter in a major hospital. I imagine that there are even more, but I just can't remember them all. My grandmother used to call me a "jack of all trades and a master of none." The experience of having so many jobs felt great to me. Somehow one position flowed right into the next in a synchronistic way. I remember many people being worried about the multitude of directions that my life had taken. Some of the conversations that I had with various people left me thinking that they considered my blackness, or gayness, or being a woman, to be the reason that "I couldn't find my way." I learned that predictable rhythms make most people comfortable. Because I was moving through my life in an unfamiliar rhythm, I was described as lacking fortitude and "stick-to-it-ive-ness," and as being selfish.

I think that I chose to "follow the string," so to speak, in my professional life because I was searching for myself in my personal life and had no known path to follow there. I was searching, not because I was lost, but because I had no idea how to bring the three pieces of myself together into one central axis that would allow me to feel whole inside. Depending on whose advice I listened to on a particular day, I would feel okay. or not okay. about who I was. Whether or not I felt proud of any of the parts of me was a direct reflection of the people and circumstances in my life at any given time. It was like being stuck in a game of "whack-a-mole." I would find comfort in being black; allow my courage to rise; own that part of myself; and then I would allow someone else's judgment to enter my consciousness and knock me down. At times when I would learn a little bit about myself as a lesbian and then be subject to someone else's lack of understanding or negative opinion, I would feel crushed time and again. I wasn't lost; just on a thirty-year journey to connect to a greater vision of my purpose and myself.

Part of my impetus for writing this is that I want you to know that it didn't need to take me thirty years to understand that my uniqueness was important and even meant to be. What I know now is that I endured so much unnecessary suffering, because as a confused teenager no one ever said to me, "You're perfect just as you are." No one ever told me that God and the Universe gave me the charge of being black, gay, and female because I needed to gain unique experiences for my future work. If only someone had said, "Cara Michele, you're here for a specific purpose and your diverse traits are your tools." Since I didn't get that message, I've taken the responsibility as an adult to bring that understanding to myself.

I want you to know that you're perfect as you are. I want you to wake up and know this, even if no one has ever told you; and know that it's your responsibility to embrace this understanding for yourself as well. Too many of us have been wandering around in pain simply because we were told that there were many things wrong with us; that we were somehow unacceptable.

The circumstances of your journey are gifts and opportunities from which you can learn more about your strength, courage and wisdom, not just for your own sake, but for the benefit of all of us. Because we are human beings breathing the same air and walking on the same ground, we are connected. We have a commonality that cannot be denied. This does not diminish the importance of our diversity within that collective. The truth of the matter is that each of us has different ways of doing things. That's what makes us able to bring so many unique perspectives to bear in identifying and solving life's problems and challenges.

At this stage of my life, people tell me how happy and peaceful I seem. Some people say that they are envious of my happiness, and want to know what they can do to find that feeling for themselves. I often chuckle a little to myself because I wonder, "If they really knew what I went through to get there, would they still be interested? Would they summon the courage to hang on to their own personal authenticity long enough to find the wisdom and purpose in it?"

The most powerful thing in the world is a resolute mind, so don't wait thirty years. Decide today, right now, that you and all your glorious differences are okay. Most importantly, never look back.

In Partnership,
Cara Michele

Cara Michele Nether is the founder of Women in Wellness, an acupuncture and eastern medicine based practice that focuses on helping women see their strength, potential and higher calling as a way of creating ease and wellness in life. By moving energy with acupuncture and exploring lifestyle options, Cara Michele partners with her clients as they create a heartfelt life of service for themselves and others. You can reach her at www.cmnether.com

Finding My Way Home: The Path of Trauma as a Path to Awakening

ANNE FRANCES MARTIN

INTRODUCTION

I remember very vividly flying out of San Francisco, eastward bound for my 25th college reunion. I was filled with a sense of dread. In the pit of my stomach was a very large knot. The question: 'What do I have to show for these 25 years?' had been playing in my mind like an old, broken phonograph record. I found myself measuring my life against that traditional 'yardstick' that goes something like this: "I am successful at age (fill in your 30, 40, 50, etc. age), if I have some combination of the following things: fulfilling marriage, beautiful children, money in the bank, successful career, mortgage on a place called home." As I headed off to my reunion, I was acutely aware I didn't have most of those things.

Writing this now, on the cusp of age 50, I still don't have many of those things. What I have come to understand, and perhaps much more slowly to appreciate, is that the life I have led, the experiences I have had, and the choices I have made, have all led me to remember who I am: that I am, that we all are, love, and that love is God. As I recognize that, I also realize for me, that is what matters. My journey has been one of incredible trauma, and also one of extraordinary healing. As a human, I would never have chosen to experience what I have experienced, and yet I do now know as soul, I have chosen precisely every experience I have had.

I am writing this for those of you whose life might also not have been so neat and tidy, for those of you who might not feel your life measures up to some traditional yardstick, and for those of you who have experienced significant trauma. My hope is that by the sharing of my story, you will in some way be supported on your own journey, to keep finding your way, to not give up on yourself or your life, and to trust your own process and its perfection, in pointing the way to your own heart, to honor your own divinity.

In sharing my story, I am choosing to break some social taboos. I do this with loving intention. I am choosing to speak out about incest in a society that largely supports secrecy and silence. I am speaking out using my given name, knowing I have family members who neither support nor affirm my experience. And while it might seem odd or contraindicative, I also want you to know this: I deeply love those family members.

I don't want to live in a world where secrets fester. Where there are parts of me, or parts of you, that we hold as shameful, bad, or ugly. I know those parts, held that way, lead to violence, gifts unexpressed, light diminished. As women and men, we cannot wake up to who we truly are and claim our full power if we honor long held pacts of secrecy and silence.

I want to live in a world where we consciously recognize that each moment of coming together as family members is a free will choice. Free from rules- no shoulds or 'have tos', free of the old paradigms of obligation and loyalty, free of projections on the other that they need us to keep silent about certain things, or to behave in certain ways. Relating in these old ways stunts our evolution, limits our self-expression, and prevents all of us from being in the full power of who we are.

And finally, I want to live in a world where all of us claim the limitlessness of who we are and fully recognize our gifts. That includes those of you who have experienced significant trauma. The story that 'you were done to', or that 'your life is over because of X', is just that, a story. Please don't get stuck there. There is so much waiting for you on the other side. But you have to be the one who chooses. You can choose to hide in the story, to numb yourself or otherwise hide from your pain, or you can summon what might seem like the tiniest speck of light within your otherwise seemingly broken heart, to begin to find your way. Your way will open for you if you do that, but the choice to take that pathway is yours and yours alone.

MY STORY

My teens and early twenties had three predominant themes: keep up appearances, seek external achievements with a vengeance, and never stop moving. I was a scholar athlete at my high school, shared top-of-the-class honors with a few of my classmates, and went on to collect degrees from Dartmouth and Stanford. Despite appearances, the signs of the secret I was keeping from myself, the secret I was keeping from the world, were very evident. I was bulimic, I plied myself with alcohol and various pharmaceuticals to try to make peace with relentless insomnia, and I puzzled over the seeming riddle: why does my outer world bless me with awards and accolades when inside all I want to do is die?

Terrified of the 'real world' and seduced by the allure of graduate fellowships, I then spent 7 years in 3 different PhD programs. While I never received a PhD, my one short stint in a psych ward yielded the greatest blessing of those years: an anti-depressant that had a soporific effect. For the first time in my life I had a stronger guarantee I would receive a full nights' sleep and I didn't have to pay the price of the bitter morning after taste of Jack Daniels or the risk of sleeping pill addiction.

The truly major turning point came one day in my early 30's in a therapy setting. Mentioning to my therapist that I had a headache and felt shaky, she intuited I might be angry, and asked if I was willing to try coloring or ripping up a phone book. Alarmed at the prospect of ripping up anything in front of someone, I accepted what seemed the lesser challenge. Grasping a large, fat, red crayon in my non-dominant, left hand, I unleashed a chaotic fury that tore the page. Ten minutes later I sat somewhat startled amidst shredded strips of pale yellow newsprint that moments before had been the local yellow pages. So began a process that gave birth to some 1200 drawings and paintings, and the memories of 18 years of sexual abuse by my father. What had felt like a hungry, empty, outer quest suddenly became a fertile, inner one.

Therapy lasted thirteen years and served as the anchor for work with three additional gifted healers who appeared synchronistically in my life one-by-one. The healing presence and touch of a body worker over 11 years of that period gave my body permission to tell its own story of the abuse, and fostered the rebirth of my innate capacity to sense, to feel, and to think consciously. An extraordinary year spent under the tutelage of a male tantra teacher transformed the deep wound I had held regarding my sexual energy and power. And a very gifted energy worker not only balanced the biochemical processes of my body but also supported me in clearing beliefs, agreements, equations, and energy patterns from this life and others that were blocking my path to wholeness.

As intense as those 13 years were, perhaps the most challenging and humbling part of the entire journey came when I returned home to my native roots of Baltimore 2 ½ years ago. Blessed by a loving community of fellow seekers and guided by an interdimensional process that allows me to identify and clear negative thought patterns, I have begun to embrace human reality with true precision and care and to find my real power. Finding that precision has meant navigating and releasing a virtual quagmire of old patterns of delusion and deception that kept me safe as a child. Underneath that old armoring, I have found the exquisite softness and beauty of an open, trusting heart, so alive and so knowing in the perfection of all things. I marvel at the gift of being able to hold the reality of the sexual abuse experience fully in my heart, on native soil, and to know it has nothing to do with who I am.

As I reflect on my words, I recognize this writing is my way of finding my way into a place of balance, where I am able to hold what in the early recognition sometimes seem like incongruous truths: I experienced eighteen years of sexual abuse; I did not choose that experience as a human, I chose that experience as a soul; I am whole, and most importantly, everything and everyone is God. My father, my mother, and I are One. While coming to these truths has been anything but easy, there has been something deeply fulfilling about staying true to my own process, trusting my life, and honoring its course. I have come to trust the exquisite perfection of all of life, and for that, I am deeply grateful. That is my yardstick, and the place I call home isn't something I need a mortgage on, it's who I am.

Anne Frances Martin. I am a life coach, a dancer, a speaker, a writer, a living foodist. Charting the territories of living in not knowing, letting the moment live me, learning to love, to be loved, to be the lover, not knowing what that means one moment to the next, knowing the contours, the shapes, of life in this moment will always be my teacher. I currently live in Baltimore, Maryland and am writing a book about my life. I can be reached at annefrancesmartin@gmail.com

Mnemosyne's Granddaughters

MARILYN F. CLARK

I invite you to open yourself to the Divine Feminine right now. Take a long, slow breath and read these words bringing them to meet the holy within yourself:

Darkness, Water, Earth, Creation,
Body, Vagina, Ovaries, Breast, Smooth Muscles
Cycles, Circles, Fullness-Emptiness
Love, Creativity, Blessing
Eggs, Pregnant, Gestation, Birth
Fruit, New Life
Miscarriage, Stillborn, Death, Transformation
Evolution, Nature
Kindness, Muse, Goddess
Gentle, Strong, Courageous
Acceptance, Receptivity
Friend, Companion
Culture, Container, Family, Ancestor
Wholeness, Completeness, Memory
add more…

Take the words, like little magnets on your refrigerator, arrange them any way you want. Play with them. Make icing, put them on cookies and eat them. Make clay sculptures of them. Write them in the sand on the beach and roll over them as the waves come in. Let them become a part of you, infusing, inspiring, awakening, and beginning a creative process.

It was April 1975 and another sunny, pleasant day in Cuernavaca, Mexico where my new husband and I were attending a month-long course at a Sufi center. However, on this day, I was feeling neither sunny nor pleasant. In an afternoon class we studied a chapter from a text that was difficult to understand leaving me feeling intimidated, left out and bored. I am a feminist and while attempting to be tolerant of the overuse of male nouns in philosophical and spiritual texts, I nevertheless became quite impatient with it that afternoon. I tired of the discussion and finding no room for myself and my experience there, I retreated, in my thoughts, to the mystery of my own body where my first child was developing moment by moment. I was experiencing with this pregnancy the true felt sense of sacred creation as new life grew inside my body. It was not a philosophical construct, but a real experience. I felt it; I knew it -- the miracle of life. In a moment, on a lazy afternoon in Mexico, I understood that divinity could be known through the feminine.

I had approached the feminine aspect of the Divine through reading about Greek and Hindu deities, but I had not experienced the Divine Feminine in the temple of my own body. The creative mystery of the continuity of life in any and all forms has been, to me, one of the surest evidences of the existence of Divine Spirit. I suddenly blurted out to the class that the 'Beloved,' the word used to kindle an intimate connection with the Divine, could be contemplated and understood through the creative mystery of woman's body. I trembled for what seemed like hours afterward as the intensity of this new knowing coursed through my being.

My husband walked with me back to our hacienda. There was a lovely jasmine bush near the door in full bloom, and I steered us to the bush where I lay down to rest and to let my body stop trembling. He smiled and caressed me. His infinite kindness surrounded me in my vulnerability. The sweet smell of jasmine soothed my trembling. Gradually I returned to equilibrium. I have never forgotten those moments, that day, the jasmine bush, my husband's love, and my deep knowing of the Divine Feminine. She was in me and I in her.

Within a short time after we returned to the United States, I found that my life path was laid down on a route that encompassed music, art, spirituality, and non-ordinary states of consciousness.

I began a training program in the Bonny Method of Guided Imagery and Music. I first discovered that even though I was not a performing musician, I could have a deeply intimate relationship with music through intentional listening. Further I learned that opening up to my inner imaginative spaces opened new avenues of creative expression for me: mandala drawing, journaling, authentic movement, musical improvisation, and mask making. These expressive avenues were fun, deep and meaningful. Throughout the training program, I was encouraged to let go of left-brain processes that judge and criticize creative expression and to give voice to non-rational, non-linear right-brain processes where creative expression resides. What freedom and release there was in that! Further, I let go of any idea that I was not worthy of good things or that someone else in my family had all the artistic talent. I dared to accept that I was creative, artistic, musical, graceful, and poetic. More freedom; more release. The pathway to my own inner creativity was cleared and opened. With hindsight I see that I was opening to the Divine Feminine and giving her expression through my self-expression. It would take years before I would use these words to describe the creative aspect of my spirituality.

In Greek mythology, the goddess Mnemosyne gave birth to the nine Muses who were fathered by Zeus. Mnemosyne's realm was

Memory. Before alphabets, Memory was what held the cultural traditions, stories, myths, healing practices, rituals and rites. She had the power of naming. Because of her, the laws of nature and the universe continued to work. Her water spirit daughters inspired the expression of creative arts. They were always welcome on Olympus. Over the centuries, in Western Europe, Greek and Roman myths gave way to the teachings of the Catholic Church. The Divine Feminine was oppressed and forgotten. Philosophers worshipped the intellect, and nature was considered a base distraction by the Church. In the 1800's, the Romantics returned to the intelligence of the senses and remembered the muses from Greek and Roman mythology. They invoked the muses through their imagination to help inspire them to bring nature, beauty, and spirit back into the world of poetry, art, and music. The male artist was said to get his inspiration from his muse, the feminine creative energy that he projected onto real or imagined women.

For women, there is no need to project beauty, creativity, or inspiration onto another. We experience it within ourselves, through our bodies' connections to lunar cycles, through the deep urge to nest and to birth. We need only lay aside the self-doubt and conditioned patterns of disempowerment to find our own eternal in-dwelling muse. We know that we have rich interior worlds that hold many, many facets. The interior castle, to borrow St. Theresa of Avila's image, provides rich exploration for us while we learn to recognize our self-worth as a positive force in the world. No longer are we embarrassed by or ashamed of our creative expression. We might not exhibit our art in galleries or publish our memoirs or novels, but we have the freedom and the right to express ourselves with as much creativity as we choose. We reclaim the memory of the goddess and awaken the muse within ourselves.

Whether you have found her or not, she resides within you, deep inside. The pearl of creativity lives within you. Emotions, cognitions, inspiration, physical prowess and strength ebb and flow with your cycles and with your years. You are creativity. You and the Muse of the Poets are one. No excuses. No time for poor sense of esteem. Not now. Claim your creativity. Did you compare yourself to someone else and disqualify yourself from ever realizing your creativity? No more disclaimers. While you may not have gone to art school, you have every right to express yourself. Take these words out of your vocabulary: "I am not an artist." Take out all of the disclaimers for the writer, actor, poet, and musician. Put in "I enjoy expressing myself. It is fun and sometimes surprisingly meaningful." Stop apologizing. Embrace your Muse. Go for walks together. Visit art museums. Go to concerts, exhibits, and plays. Take a pocket size notebook with you because she's going to start talking to you, showing you things you never noticed before and you want to remember what she's teaching you about how she sees, hears and feels the world around both of you.

Mnemysome and her daughters are alive and thriving, helping you to reclaim your creativity. Remember them, Granddaughter. Listen to yourself and express what and who you are. This is your birthright!

Marilyn F. Clark, licensed psychotherapist, uses music and imagery to help persons tap their deepest potentials. An experienced workshop leader and teacher, she has worked with people throughout the United States and Europe. Marilyn has studied the Bonny Method of Guided Imagery and Music with Helen Bonny, the Usui System of Reiki Healing, the Great Round of Mandala, mysticism, and storytelling. She dreams that women hold the promise of an evolving planet within their hearts. Marilyn lives in Baltimore, MD and can be contacted at marilynclark@mac.com

PART TWO

I Co-create with Others

A Life Lived In Sisterhood

DOTTI DRUMM

Mine has been a life lived in sisterhood... in the beginning by circumstances of birth and a neglecting father, but since then by choice. The riches of my life have been derived from or enhanced by my close relationships with women.

My alcoholic father had little time for me. When he was not ignoring me, he was clearly demonstrating his preference for my older sister, even declaring on occasion that I was not his daughter. He finally drank himself to death when I was six.

My strong-willed mother, toughened by her experience of the Depression, was determined she and her two daughters would not return to the inner city poverty she had left years before. Though Baltimore in the early 60's only offered her work of the menial sort, she found work, we were able to keep our house, and she provided the basic necessities. My mother and sister were the foundation of my life for the next several years, and we thrived.

My earliest chosen sister was Charlene. I had moved into the neighborhood when I was four, and she lived across the street. She was intense, energetic and curious - everything the imaginative, creative, slightly shy soul that I was, could ask for in a playmate. We were instant friends and spent hours every day running, dreaming and playing like revelers in the carnival of life. Looking back, I can see that being with Char and remembering how we related and how we got each other through scary and challenging times, would set a pattern for my life. With the help of friends, girls and women, I could face doubt and emerge free and aware.

Char and I played outside when the weather permitted, and if not, we were in my basement. One such day my mom and Char's mom went shopping, and we were left with my father as our "sitter". We were in the basement enjoying our domestic pretend-cooking when we suddenly heard a loud thud. I called out for my dad, but heard no response.

Char and I ran up the stairs and tried to open the door, but found it would not budge. I pounded on the door, called for my father, and started to panic. Charlene kept her cool, even though we were only five years old. She said that the two of us had to push on the door steadily until we could move it a smidgen and see what was blocking it. It was difficult, but we persevered.

Finally, we were able to get the door open enough to put an arm through and feel what was blocking the door. It was my dad. He had passed out and fallen in front of the basement door. He would not respond. Char and I decided to continue to push at the door hoping we could move him enough to squeeze through the opening. After much effort, we managed the task.

We shook my dad many times in an effort to wake him up, but to no avail. So we sat on the couch, trying to decide what to do next. My mother came home to find us sitting there. She called the doctor, my dad was put in the hospital, and he never came home. He died 13 days later.

Despite my father's legacy, and despite the training I later received at my Catholic elementary school, I slowly developed my confidence and learned to rely on my inner strength and vision. I found myself refusing many times to conform to the petty rules and impositions of the nuns at my school, and being frequently punished for insolence and "loose" morality. Yet, no matter how hard they tried to move me to their point of view, the good "sisters" couldn't overcome my sense that the life they portrayed as proper, good and spiritual was totally lacking in beauty, purpose and substance.

I knew somewhere deep inside I was destined to be more than just a married woman, either to Christ or man, humbly obeying and sacrificing to the whims and priorities of somebody else's expectation of me. I could sense instead that what was truly expected of me was to break free of the conventions of family, school and church. I refused to relinquish my knowing that only by confidently becoming what I truly am would I be able to live the life I was intended to live.

Thankfully, my mother couldn't afford to send us to Catholic high school, so I ended up going to the local public school. On that first day of classes I entered the building, expectant, nervous and hopeful.

It was there that I met Bean. Like Char helped me push open the door of the basement, she was to be one of those "sisters" who helped me move toward freedom. Bean was very different from anyone else I had ever known. She was truly her own person – natural, spontaneous, comfortable with herself and confident without being arrogant. She was never bothered by any concern of what other people thought of her, and yet she was never aloof. It seemed more like others impressions and opinions of her never even entered her consciousness.

I remember the first time I went to her house. As I walked in, her mom said, "She's downstairs. Go on down". Following her instructions, I found Bean in the bathtub shaving her legs. I sat on the toilet, and we talked. It seemed as natural to her as if we were sitting out on the porch, while it took me a little while to relax into the conversation. But it was indeed only a little while, as we quickly became fast friends.

Here was someone I could be myself with. Here was someone willing to take me as I was. In fact, as time went on, I found that if I tried to be different, cautious or defensive with her, I would suddenly feel like a fake even when she didn't say a word about it. Somehow her presence made it easier for me to drop all my pretenses, and just be who and what I was at that point in time.

About a year into our friendship, Bean got a job at American Handicrafts, a chain of stores that provided material and kits for people interested in making their own things from baskets to jewelry to sculptures. Because she was on staff, she would bring home samples of crafts to do, and we would spend hours doing foil art, wood-burning, transfers and beadwork. We had a blast and discovered ways to make all sorts of different artwork together. Neither one of us had any preconceived idea of the "proper" way of doing these crafts; so we explored, experimented and experienced.

That love of discovering new creative ways to express ourselves went on for years and took many forms. We did tombstone rubbings in an old cemetery in Rhode Island, wrote and published a pamphlet exploring the stories behind historical markers on the route to Ocean City, Maryland, and every Christmas for years we made and decorated dough ornaments. To this day, when I try new mediums and methods in my artwork, I feel the joy of exploring and creating with Bean, a freedom to create newness that we shared in the context of true friendship.

Sisterhood remains an important window and mirror for me as I continue in adulthood to embrace and explore my emerging self. This bond led me to home school my son with like-minded women and it's guided me to pass this wisdom onto the next generation of girls/women by showing them the value in the bonds of sisterhood.

Dotti Drumm *lives in Baltimore, Md. She is the mother of two grown children. She is a self-taught artist, using reclaimed and recycled materials. Her work can be found at local shows and at the American Folk Art Museum in NY.*

You can view some of Dotti's art work at:
indiepublic.com/profile/DottiDrumm

She can be contacted at drobot121@yahoo.com

The Little Voice

KELLY LUNDAHL

It has taken me many years but I am finally doing it. I am listening to the little voice. I have been hearing the little voice my whole life. Now I am paying attention.

As a little girl of five or so, living in a tiny rural Maine town, we had a black shepherd mix that loved me with a fierceness that kept the dog in the house when friends came over to play. Nellie had never hurt anyone, but she did not like kids near me and strangers were out of the question.

One day, while I was playing in the yard, a new mailman came strolling down the road and onto our property. The lazing dog jumped to her feet and watched him intently. The little voice had me clutch a handful of the shepherd's fur as she bristled at his approach. I stood patiently with my fingers deep in her hair as he walked by. She wouldn't leave the yard, so when he passed into the neighbor's yard, I let go of her and went back to play. Standing on the porch steps, my father had been waiting with baited breath for fear that if he said something I would be startled, look at him and worse, let go. He often recounts the story with a funny feeling of awe that I knew what to do without being told and that the dog twice my size obeyed the fingers on her back.

As I grew up, the little voice kept me company. It comforted me and talked me out of revenge when the neighbor girl and her friends played beauty parlor with my doll and cut off all her hair. It kept me from hanging out with my friends who shoplifted at the drug store.

As my teenage years progressed, a tension grew between the little voice and me. At times, it was a nagging irritant that seemed to order me around. Screaming "Shut up!" rarely quieted it, and I often came home furious that I couldn't ignore it.

During our senior year of high school, my best friend Denise and I went to visit my brother in Helena, a hundred miles from our current home town of Great Falls. It was a big road trip with the promise of fun. After my brother went to work that Friday afternoon we made plans to double date his neighbors, two young men who acted like they knew my brother well. We were thrilled that they liked us, as they were impressively older, at almost 20. We left my brother a note and headed out in a big new pick-up truck that made them seem all- the- more mature. After a quick dinner, we went on a country drive to see where one of the boys worked with horses. Could it get better for me? Cute boys and horses! The little voice was pushed away without a listen.

The date went bad when the driver, Denise's date, decided that she was a tease and had better put out now. Why did we think they wanted to date us? The spineless boy whom I had kissed didn't say a word. With my arm around my crying friend, I told them to take us home. I was scared, but the little voice was strong.

There was a price for transportation, the driver told us. With my refusal, we were dumped out, and the truck tore away in a whirl of dust and gravel. Thirty miles out in the middle of the Montana prairie my little voice didn't say, "I told you so." It told me to be calm and that we could sort this out and get home safely. The little voice spoke reassuring words directly to my friend and stopped her hysterical sobbing.

We headed toward a single light that gleamed in the distance. After walking nearly an hour toward that light a truck came roaring up behind us. The quiet boy came driving back to retrieve us. His hostile buddy allowed the ride while verbally abusing us. As a wordless presence, the little voice accompanied us, as I remained poised and alert for future danger. We came back to my frightened, angry pacing brother who, though much louder than the voice, was nowhere near as powerful.

The little voice kept talking. I listened with varying degrees of attentiveness. It kept me shoveling the little old neighbors' walks in the winter and mowing their grass in the summer. Staying out of Denise's friend's car one night kept us safe from harm. The little voice was worried. "Stay home, stay home" was the mantra. Though I yearned to go to the field party and had gone before, Denise, the little voice, and I stayed home. After a night of drinking around a bon-fire, Wendy, Denise's friend, drove her car off an embankment and was killed. We sorrowed long for that girl. I wondered about that little voice.

A number of years passed before I could fully comprehend that the voice wasn't an irritant or a fun wrecker. It was wise. And as I listened more attentively, the voice got softer.

A few years ago, after marriages, children, time, and long distances, Denise called me to say she had been diagnosed with ALS, the dreaded Lou Gehrig's disease. We cried over the terrible prognosis. Words poured from my mouth to tell her that I would come as soon as I could. After hanging up, I panicked. What could I possibly say to her and her family? The little voice reassured me that I would know what to say when the time came. For two years, I flew out to spend time with her every three or four months, every time wondering how I could be of help. Almost two years later, knowing it would be my last visit, the little voice told me I had things to say to Denise as well as to her daughters, husband, and mom. "What was that to be?" I asked the little voice, horrified. "You'll know when you get there, and don't worry."

I did worry. Until I got there, I worried a lot. But after I got there, I turned my worries over to the little voice and told it to do the talking. Opportunities arose for me to spend time with each of those hurting people, and words came from me that were not my own. I walked away from each of those moments at peace and in awe of what the little voice said, knowing that I could never come near the wisdom that it had shared. I don't remember what was said; just that it wasn't me talking. The little voice provided me with comfort and gave it to others.

The little voice speaks quietly now. Perhaps it is more a part of me. I find that when I let the little voice do the talking, I am freer, happier, and more peaceful than ever. The little voice says more meaningful things than I can on my own. So now, I consciously try to not only listen to the little voice, but also let that voice be my voice. In those times, I know the presence of God. The feeling of being a tool or a vessel makes me feel like I am a good part of a great thing, and my heart soars.

Kelly Lundahl *lives in Baltimore, Md. with her husband and son. She is a graphic artist who homeschools her son and teaches History, Writing and Art in a homeschooled co-op.*

The Accidental Evolutionary Woman

MARCIA MERRILL

Education has always been an important part of my life. I hold a Bachelor's degree in modern language and linguistics, a Master's in Education in instructional systems development/bilingual and bicultural education, a Master's in counseling and psychology, and Certifications in my chosen field, career/life counseling and transitioning.

As you can see, education is a huge part of who I am...

But when Andrea Hylen told me how Evolutionary Women (EW), something that was more about spirituality, had changed her life, I have to admit that I was intrigued.

I've always been a "big picture" type of thinker. I'm analytical and detail-oriented. I see the forest and the trees! So it's no surprise that I initially thought that EW was something that wouldn't be part of an educated woman's experience.

After hearing Andrea's ringing endorsement, I was actually thinking about attending an EW retreat. If someone had told me 20 years ago that I would be doing this, I would have told them they were crazy. Back then, I would have thought that concepts like "energy healing" were more "out there" or "woo woo." These ideas were something that, at the time, wasn't me.

Over the years, I have grown and changed. In my work and life, I had always believed in having a positive attitude. I may not have used the same terms that EW and others did, but I did share these beliefs.

I still didn't think it was something for an "educated woman" like me. Boy, was I wrong…

When I decided to attend an EW weekend retreat, I really didn't know what to expect. I knew that I wanted to interact with more women. And, let's be real here, I thought it was a good business decision too.

As I said, I had already strongly believed in the power of positive thinking and the existence of positive energy. Maybe this is what got me to go.

Or maybe it was because having been a Career/Life Transitions Coach with more than 20 years of experience, I had seen my clients transform their lives simply by learning something new. Maybe I could learn something new too.

The retreat, I was told, would include spending a weekend with 40 to 50 other midlife women who cared about creating a more peaceful, loving planet. That sounded good to me, and a weekend retreat sounded nice.

One of the many surprises of the weekend was that these women would turn out to be like-minded folks—not just with themselves, but with me. Before going, I didn't realize that I was like-minded. I just didn't know.

And the word "nice" didn't begin to describe my life changing experience. Since attending that first retreat, I've been to others, and they've all greatly influenced my life. I was so surprised…

EW's co-founders Bonnie Kelley and Lucky Sweeny were inspired and influenced by Barbara Marx Hubbard, a highly intelligent, educated Ph.D, evolutionary visionary. Barbara spoke to my educated mind, yet, more importantly, Evolutionary Women spoke to my heart. EW gave me a safe place to explore my spirituality and gave me a place to think about the bigger question of spirituality—how we go about living our lives and live our values.

I already was open-minded; if I hadn't been, I wouldn't have gone to that initial retreat in the first place. I certainly wouldn't have gotten anything out of it, that's for sure.

I discovered that I have so much more in common with other Evolutionary Women than I ever could have imagined!

I met so many cool women from all over the country--teachers, psychologists, healers, peace ministers, and everyday women who cared. They were all showing up and taking a stand.

And I've kept in touch with a number of them—through e-mail and EW's Light Pages. I was invited to join a local spirituality book group. I did, and the camaraderie and loving energy that we share is such an important part of my life.

EW started me on a spiritual path--not one of organized religion. I emphasize this because I know many may worry that EW is too "new age-y." This isn't the case at all! Jews, Muslims, Christians, and Agnostics alike go to EW, and its beliefs resonate with all of us.

Any woman who believes in a higher purpose and creating with others (co-creating as Barbara Marx Hubbard, the Founder would say) is an Evolutionary Woman--she just may not realize it yet.

That's how it was for me--a huge "Aha!" I felt like I was home.

The entire weekend was a learning/growing experience for me. Earnest conversations with my roommate, the leaders, and the women in the Art Room; the laughter, camaraderie, and in-depth talks we had; the energy and positive feelings were so wonderful.

I learned, through the retreats, that like-minded voices spoke with joy and were united in the belief that we can make a difference in this world, and we need to do so. And I realized that the women believe, like I do, that the world is part of an abundant universe!

Abundance, being loving and caring about others, and being dedicated to co-creating peace on the planet were all themes of the EW retreat. They were also things that are so important to me.

I realized that for quite some time, I was an Evolutionary Woman, and I didn't know it!

All of my clients, both former and current, know I'm all about abundance, cooperation (collaboration not competition), and bringing positive energies and attitudes in all that we do, say, or think. Now, they (both women and men) all look forward to when I will attend my next retreat because they know that I will talk with them about EW and the philosophies of co-creation.

Besides all this, I realize that there is more to me than being a Career/Life Transitions Coach. I love my work, and it is my passion. But it's just one of them. As I continue down my spiritual path on my journey through life, I know I have a greater purpose as well. Although I don't know what it is right now, that's okay.

Evolutionary Women was a catalyst for me to embrace my spirituality and to incorporate it in all aspects of my life. I've made many great friends, and I look forward to where the next steps in life will take me. I was the Accidental Evolutionary Woman.

But we all know that there are no such things as accidents…

Marcia Merrill, AKA The Transition Chick, is a Career/Life Transitions Coach and Founder of www.eCareerCorner.com. Marcia brings over 20 years of experience. An author/speaker/facilitator, Marcia is a lifelong learner! Her passion is to help midlife women fall in love with their lives and their work (in that order!). She works with career transitioners, solo-entrepreneurs, and folks not knowing "what they want to be when they grow up." You can get your FREE Transition Triumph Toolkit and get Marcia's newsletter chockfull of valuable info as a bonus at www.eCareerCorner.com. Check out Marcia's family of web sites: www.innercirclecoachinggym.com, www.transitiontriumph.com, and www.marciamerrill.com

Living As If You Are Powerful Beyond Measure

BETSY MCMAHAN

Recognizing the power of my thoughts was the first step in realizing I could play a significant role in creating the life I wanted to experience. As I began to grasp the possibility of such power, fear and disbelief popped up. Who was I kidding? Who was I to think that, as one of over 6 billion people on this planet, I actually had a hand in creating my life, not to mention the world, as we know it? Playing the role of victim was so much more appealing than taking the responsibility for all my experiences, good and bad.

Whatever you choose to call the higher power - God, Spirit, Source, Universe – I now believe this power is always with me. It's there to listen, communicate, guide and help me manifest my heart's desires. I've realized the process is actually a co-creation. This Source manifests what I put my attention on. When I focus on health and prosperity, it helps me create health and prosperity. When I focus on lack and disappointment, more of that is created.

It's amazing how God speaks to us through "coincidences." As I began feeling more empowered, I was introduced to an insightful passage written by Marianne Williamson for her book, *A Return To Love:*

Reflections on the Principles of A Course in Miracles.
"Our deepest fear is not that we are inadequate.
Our deepest fear is that we are powerful beyond measure.
It is our light, not our darkness, that most frightens us.
We ask ourselves, Who am I to be brilliant, gorgeous, talented, fabulous?
Actually, who are you not to be?
You are a child of God. Your playing small does not serve the world.
There's nothing enlightened about shrinking
so that other people won't feel insecure around you.
We are all meant to shine, as children do.
We were born to make manifest the glory of God that is within us.
It's not just in some of us; it's in everyone.
And as we let our own light shine,
we unconsciously give other people permission to do the same.
As we're liberated from our own fear,
our presence automatically liberates others."

I began to embrace the possibility. Maybe I was powerful. Maybe if I let go of fear, I could do magnificent things. What could happen if I chose to let my light shine? What if I opened up to seeing all the ways God was working in my life? Might I be surprised and realize we're in this togther? Little by little, Divine Presence made a believer out of me. I now know that my Source and I are in a constant state of communing, imaging, creating and appreciating.

Here are a few stories I remember fondly from my journey. My hope is that they inspire you to new possibilities.

COMMUNICATION OR COINCIDENCE?

I live my life in a constant dialog with Source. It's not that I hear a voice in my head; for me it's more like a knowingness that sweeps over me.

After making a decision, a feeling of peace resonates within me. Early on, it was hard to trust the feelings. I wanted to hear a voice or have a conversation. I wanted to know I wasn't making it up. Then one day I started asking for signs. From that moment, Source began "speaking" to me through license plates. Most times the messages were warm and fuzzy as if God was saying, "Have a nice day." Other times, they were directed toward specific events. For example, as I was driving to an energy healing class, I saw the license plate "OUCHFXR" – Ouch Fixer. On another occasion, I was wondering about a potential business opportunity. A moment later I saw the license plate "ITL FLY." Driving along thinking about a special someone I saw "4EVRM8S" - Forever Mates - on a car identical to his.

The most memorable message appeared on a day I was very upset. I still remember exactly where I was but can't remember why I was upset. I was sobbing. While driving, I raised my hands to the heavens and said aloud, "I give up!" Believe it or not, the very next car that drove by had the license plate, "NVRGVUP" - Never Give Up! I was amazed and responded, "Ok, but I'm gonna need a little help!"

Knowing what an important role license plates played in my spiritual journey, you can understand my desire to have a vanity tag of my own. My hope is if a person is having a particularly challenging day, they'll feel a bit better seeing my license plate. My plate reads, "U R LVD" - You Are Loved!

TRUSTING YOUR INNER GUIDANCE

One evening I stopped at the neighborhood Wal-Mart to see if there was anything I just couldn't live without. I grabbed my change purse, put my keys inside and attached my cell phone to it. As I entered, I suddenly had an overwhelming thought I was going to be robbed. As a 30-something female wearing heels, dress and pearls, I'm sure I looked like an easy mark.

As I entered, I was anxious and very alert to my surroundings. An hour ticked by and my cart became full. I felt comfortable again; the fear had lifted. So much so, I put my wallet in the cart and covered it up with a large plastic plant. (OK, I admit that wasn't very smart but I was a co-creator in this whole process.)

The next thing I did to help this enlightening experience unfold was to leave my cart at the end of an aisle, a little more than an arm's length away. As I was deciding which item to purchase, something caught my attention. I was guided to look back at my cart. Instantly I realized my change purse was gone! And with it, my license, cash, credit cards, cell phone and keys. (Later I realized there was a diamond bracelet in it as well!)

Instinctively, I wheeled my cart into the next aisle. There was a very large, scary looking man standing there. I hadn't seen him take my wallet but absolutely knew he had it. At that moment, I felt no fear. Believe it or not, I walked right up to him and said, "Excuse me, my wallet is missing and I think you have it." He looked at me and said, "Lady, I don't have your wallet" and moved down the aisle. I was persistent and said again, "I can't go anywhere without my wallet and keys. Please give them back to me." He responded "Lady, leave me alone" and walked into another aisle. I continued following as he turned and said, "Lady, you're bothering me. Stop following me. I don't have your stuff." He picked up his pace but my cart and I stayed right with him. As he turned to say something else, I glimpsed my multi-colored change purse tucked under his arm inside his jacket. I screamed, "You do have my wallet!" I grabbed his jacket with my left hand and reached for my wallet with my right. Everyone looked at me in disbelief as I recovered my things and he ran toward the rear of the store.

Who would have thought this man would be a co-creator in my life? I'm certainly glad this story had a happy ending but am just as thrilled that he helped me recognize I can trust my inner voice. I also realized I'm in control of my experiences and can choose to not be a victim. I now understand there's guidance available to me 24/7 if I'm open to receiving it.

MANIFESTING YOUR HEART'S DESIRE

Living in a state of excited expectation allows Source to help us co-create what we later experience as "reality" in our day-to-day lives. I'm a believer in making lists. Not lists of "things to do" but lists of what I choose to manifest in my life. My belief is that the list helps me clarify what I really want. The next step is to visualize the item or situation as if it has already manifested. The final step is to feel grateful for it's being in my life even before it is. I've used this technique many times – for new homes, cars, jobs and relationships. It really works! One incredible example of this happened when my mother and I created a list for a perfect living space to share. We wanted a home on the beach. We wanted to rent with an option to buy. It needed to have separate living areas for each of us so we could live together and have privacy. In total, there were 25-30 items on the list. The last item I added was a hammock. Two days later, mother and I walked through the perfect home. As we explored each area, we checked items off our list. We were sold when we opened the back door and found a hammock sitting in the backyard. Amazed and thrilled, we signed the lease!

Rev. Betsy McMahan (Lakshmi)

Betsy McMahan and her mother, Ginny Vaughn, are manifesting the life of their dreams by sharing Shaklee (www.shaklee.net/heartsanddreams). For a free copy of their book, Healthy Women, visit www.heartsanddreams.com

Betsy is also an inter-faith minister specializing in Spiritual Counseling. She especially enjoys officiating at weddings in the Baltimore area. She can be contacted via email (mcmahanb@yahoo.com). Swami Shankarananda of the Divine Life Church is her enlightened guru.

Visit www.divinelifechurch.org for more information about the Universalist perspective.

"When Life Gives You Lemons..."

LAVONNE REES

My husband passed away when I was twenty-two. Grief left me feeling frightened, vulnerable and angry that all my dreams had been lost.

For several years, I struggled in an emotional fog trying to reclaim my dreams. I was just going through the motions, doing what it took to get through each day. It was easier to let others decide how I should act and how I should speak and what truth I should show the world.

Nevertheless, the day finally came when I made a conscious choice to reclaim my voice and to live my authentic self.

My journey began unknowingly as I listened to a girlfriend share her story of being a new mom, facing career choices and feeling invisible when she saw her reflection in the mirror. I discovered a need to share my own story in a way I hoped would support, empower and embrace her. I admitted that after my husband passed, I did not know who I was or what my interests were. I let the titles I had allowed myself to wear define who I was. I had lost track of my sense of self.

I advised her that no matter what choices she was facing, she should strive to be true to herself always and not be caught up in what other people thought she should be. The best thing she could do for her family was to recognize her reflection again by rekindling her interests and sharing who she was with her family and her community. These sacred words were spoken through me for both of us; I believe they were inspired by the Sacred Divine as a reminder to me that I, too, had a voice inside of me waiting to get out. On that day, I made a conscious choice to find my joy and let my life begin again.

The amazing thing about starting with a fresh palette and not allowing others to define you is that you are totally free to create yourself. I started my journey of self-discovery at my local community schools. The first class I chose was an introduction to massage therapy. I could learn massage, help others with their physical ailments and be guaranteed at least one free massage a week. It could not get much better than that.

I truly had no concept of where that first class would lead me. During the next four years, I took every holistic healing class I could find. With each class, I felt a rebirth of joy that had died with my husband. I found a community that helped me define who I wanted to be. I learned and I taught. I healed, and I was healed. I shared my voice and I listened. I fully believe that personal touch and energy work saved my life by keeping my essence connected with the whole of life. Learning to be in touch through physical connection brought me in touch with my intuition. When I allowed inner joy to be exposed, I found within me vulnerability and a trust so deep that words do not describe it.

This is not a call for you to learn holistic healing. It is about the process of finding your authentic self. I found my joy within holistic healing. What is important is that you find your own personal joy whether it be cooking, meditation, painting, or bird watching. Whatever it is, do it as often as you can.

Joy itself will assist you in finding inner peace and tranquility. When your heart is full of joy, love and enthusiasm, you start to want to share it with others. In the process of sharing and acting on your personal truth, others get to see who you really are. It is inspirational. The result is fewer conversations of superficial fluff, and more insight into each other's essence. On paper, it may not sound like much, but just think about how often people hide behind what they think others want to see. What a world we could co-create if everyone could be completely comfortable showing and living his or her true spirit.

I took on a leadership role and began facilitating Women's circles and retreats, to breathe into existence the hidden reflection of the forgotten "other" woman inside each of us. It was important for me to bring women of like minds and priorities together to support one another. We all have dreams for our children, our planet, and ourselves. Yet, it is often hard to find space where we feel safe to communicate those desires and concerns and to manifest dreams into action.

Finding my joy allowed me to share my experiences with my "sisters," and we inspired each other to recognize our authentic reflection in the mirror once again. I saw the strength, power and wisdom that women have as they shared their stories.

The purpose of organizing retreats was and is to provide a sacred environment that creates a place to let loose. It is where we are free to support and be supported in any challenge or dream that surfaces. Within this "sanctuary," every idea and every woman has equal merit. Each woman has the opportunity to share all of her magnificence, wisdom and life experiences. An unbreakable bond is formed by doing exercises that make us think and define ourselves and by sharing our stories. During each retreat, we hold a ceremony to bless the waters and the ultimate mother, Mother Earth. This ties our individual essence to the whole. We are always rewarded with many blessings in return

As you start down your own path to find and fully live the life that gives you joy, I suggest that you find a group of women with whom you can identify and share your heart's desires. It is the very nature of women to nurture each other with compassion, empathy, and celebration. The physical manifestations that come from sharing your needs, concerns and visions within a circle of women are truly incredible. It helped me become comfortable in listening to my own inner voice and to follow my spiritual guide's signs as they were presented to me. I have such gratitude for being part of that process and for seeing my reflection in their eyes.

In my gratitude, I continually ask myself how I can co-create my heaven on earth. Each conversation within me comes back to the same ideal I have been manifesting in everything I do. It is the sharing of joy and love.

It is my desire that everyone treat themselves with kindness and genuine love and express the joy that it brings by treating all who cross their path with honor and respect. Express your joy by extending your hand, giving a smile or a kind word and making someone's day. Pass the joy, kindness and love around, one person at time. Let it spread like an infection. Grow like a tree. Together we are co-creating a world where everyone can live their truth and be accepted for their authentic selves.

In closing, I would like to share that I found joy in writing my story. I believe my love of writing is a gift obtained from my father. He loved to write letters sharing his story with his loved ones. I wish I had the foresight to keep more of them. Therefore, in honor of my father I will share a few words he often spoke. Rather than saying goodbye, he would say instead, "See you in the funny papers."

LaVonne is a facilitator of Goddess Retreats, Massage Therapist (CMT), Reiki Practitioner and Teacher, Shaklee Independent Distributor, titles that do not truly do her justice. She is innately a nurturer and pours her love for Mother Earth and Humankind into every project. LaVonne is a sister, wife, friend in the purest sense of each of these words.

She can be reached via email at sedonacalling@yahoo.com or http:/www.myspace.com/goddessretreats

Deep Longing:
A Sexual Evolution

MEGAN WOOLEVER

An intuitive counselor once told me, "Megan, you think you need to be Super Woman...so capable, totally together, absolutely invincible. But no one can relate to her. She is totally intimidating. Your true super power comes from when you show who you really are by making yourself open, vulnerable, human."

The lyrics, "I can bring home the bacon, fry it up in a pan..." ran through my head. "Wait a second," I thought to myself, "I am proud of being Super Woman. She lived through a lot. She accomplished a lot. She is a survivor!"

How could he ask this of me? Doesn't he know I am a victim of domestic violence...twice?! The very people I trusted beat me down; husband, authority figures, religious leaders. How in the world can I be vulnerable when I have to protect myself from the potentially scary, untrustworthy people out there?

Yet I knew he spoke the truth. I may have survived, but I was also empty. Wasn't that the reason I was there getting an intuitive relationship reading from him in the first place? I had to face the painful fact that to step into what I truly wanted, a healthy relationship, I needed to learn to let go of my protective Super Woman façade and soften.

And, heck, I wanted to be more than just a survivor. I wanted to thrive! I wanted to take all the pain I endured and make some sense out of it. Put simply, I wanted to evolve.

THE LONGING BEGINS

For as far back as I can remember I have longed for my Other, a partner who would complete me, activate me, see the true essence of me and celebrate it. I desired a partnership with someone that I not only loved and trusted, but also who evoked the radiant goddess that was buried deep inside me. But who? And where?

As a child I didn't understand my longing in quite those terms, but I did feel a desire, a longing that compelled me to look for someone to love. I knew this feeling was magical, otherworldly, and I was determined to find out why.

I must have seemed just like every other boy-crazy girl. But I knew I was on the hunt for nothing less than the One who would awaken me, be my soul mate. To complicate matters, I was raised with a strict religious upbringing that taught me to "save it" for my husband, because sex bonds you, ties you to someone energetically forever. So I waited. And waited. And waited. On into high school and through college, I pined away for this special someone to whom I would connect my soul, give myself. I placed all my faith in a God of love who would bring him to me.

CONFUSING SEX WITH LOVE

As a young adult I rarely dated, occasionally having a boyfriend for short periods of time, but always breaking it off before it got serious because he wasn't "the one." And the rare times when my longing felt matched, I scared them off with my intensity. I became jaded, angry, frustrated. It seemed like everyone else around me was falling in love at the drop of a hat. I asked myself, "If this is so special and natural, why is it so easy for other people to find love, but so painful and difficult for me?"

I was 22 and in graduate school when I finally said, "To hell with waiting; I'm just going to do it." After the years of holding out for "the one," I had lost hope. I gave up my faith in love and in God. So I found the first guy that came along and had sex with him, thinking, "It's just a physical act, nothing more." Much to my dismay, the emotional yearning I had built up for so long wanted more than just a physical release. Everything I understood about the energetic intimacy of sex meant that I shouldn't be sharing that kind of connection with someone that I didn't really care about. I was wholly unprepared for the massive influx of energy and information that being physically intimate with another person stirred up inside of me. So I determined to make "Mr. Right Now" into "Mr. Right." I did the only thing I could think of to legitimize myself—I married him.

That's when things got ugly. He turned abusive. I got hurt. I ran away. He threatened to kill me. I hid. I longed for love. I found sex instead. For years I repeated this pattern of longing for love and getting sex. After a second relationship turned abusive, something inside finally shifted. I heard a still, small voice say, "Megan, slow down and figure this out or you will keep repeating this experience."

I am an intuitive, empathic person, and my boundaries with people had always been a bit negotiable. I realized that I had mistaken physical intimacy for spiritual and emotional intimacy, trying to find a way to love the men I had sex with because I felt energetically connected to them. I became enmeshed in their world and lost myself. I needed to learn to be both an individual identity and a collaborative, universal consciousness. I needed to move back and forth between being in my own, unique energy system and being in the merged field of intimate lovers.

I wanted a relationship badly, but what I'd been doing was shutting down and putting walls up around myself because of all the pain I'd experienced. That's when I visited my intuitive counselor friend. He urged me to let go, to soften and open. Thus began my journey of conscious evolution.

CONSCIOUSLY UNPACKING MY SEXUALITY

I began by cultivating an awareness and appreciation for sex and love in myself. I questioned my motives, my beliefs and assumptions, the ways in which I had protected myself from being hurt or disappointed by closing myself off. Why was sex so powerful? Where did this impulse come from?

I gave myself permission to own my desire to be in a co-creative relationship. Instead of being ashamed of my longing like it was a weakness, I celebrated it as an expression of being uniquely me. And I determined that if I had this desire, I might not be the only one; there must be someone else out there that could match my passion.

I began a study regimen. I read everything I could find on tantra, sacred sexuality, kundalini, bisexuality, polygamy, sexual healing and magic. I studied my body through massage, energy work, yoga, and sexual chi kung. I experimented with my sexuality in safe, contained ways that oriented to my own energy system. I began to practice the art of self-love.[I] I learned about the subtle body layers, energy centers and how permeable we all really are. I began to understand more about global consciousness and our collective awareness as a planet.

By following my intuition, I began to experiment with techniques that drew my sexual energy upwards through the energy centers (chakras) in my body to awaken my God potential. I aroused the raw sexual energy associated with the base of my spine, the kundalini, and began to move that energy upwards, refining it as I drew it upwards into each chakra until it opened at my crown.[II] I found it took on a distinct perspective and had a unique emanation as it mixed with the energies of each individual chakra.

I discovered that the sexual arousal energy inside of me was some of the most potent and powerful creative energy possible and that it could be used and directed for healing, growth and transformation. I learned what it feels like to channel orgasmic energy towards an intention, a thought-form, and have it manifest. I began to see just how important my self-practice was to strengthening and aligning my system to my essential self.

Eventually, my self-love practice had developed a strong enough sexual energy body that I felt that I could practice with another person without losing myself. I took a lover and experienced a spontaneous kundalini awakening during sex. During orgasm the pathway I had been tenderly cultivating shot like a lightening bolt up my spine. It opened my heart wider than it had ever been opened before, and I was able to love without conditions or expectations, to embody love as a way of being. When my lover went away, I determined to keep my heart open to flowing love, redirecting it in a broader way to the world at large instead of one person. I broke wide open and let my self-protection dissolve.

STEPPING INTO CO-CREATIVE INTIMACY

I knew that staying single and continuing to unfold on my own was useful, safe and enjoyable, but I also knew that the greatest evolutionary journey I could take was with a life-partner. I was ready to take this creative potential to the next level and amplify it, to go to the unexplored territories that could be better accessed in a co-creative relationship charged with sexual energy. I called into my life a sacred lover, a husband, to heal and teach me about being in a loving, committed, conscious relationship.

To this day I am still challenged to soften and let go to be in conscious creation with him. I am keenly aware now that the loving of another person is an ongoing practice of healing wounds by letting go of judgment and staying open, vulnerable. We have had to let go of who we are, our old protection stories, to open to who we are to become.

When two people come together in sexual union, they harness the creative power of God. Today we co-create the great work, the journey of embodying our universal self, our God consciousness, as a couple. [III] Ours is a spiritual partnership, committed to reminding each other daily of our God essence, especially during painful times when we get triggered and forget. Through loving someone who woos my essential self to the surface, I have the opportunity to remember who I truly am. I am encouraged and challenged daily to consciously embody my true essence. My deepest longing is finally fulfilled. For I have found the God of love, and she is me.

Megan Woolever *is a Healer, Teacher and Evolutionary Catalyst in the San Francisco Bay Area. Her practice is Emerge Healing and specializes in Personal Transformation and Self-Evolution. She incorporates Energy Healing, Hypnotherapy, Life Coaching, Bodywork, and Intuitive Guidance to help you shift from being stuck to being struck by the magnificence of who you truly are. Visit www.emergehealing.com or call 415.652.8004 to schedule a free 15-minute phone consultation.*

[I] I highly recommend Betty Dodson's *Sex for One: The Joy of Selfloving* as a means for understanding and exploring selfloving.

[II] For more information on how to refine your sexual energy towards personal healing and transformation I recommend Mantak Chia's *The Multi-Orgasmic Woman: Discover Your Full Desire, Pleasure and Vitality.*

[III] *Tantra: The Art of Conscious Loving* by Charles and Caroline Muir was instrumental in helping to shape my vision for a conscious sexual partnership.

Conversations with Mother/Father God... My Universal Self

MARILYN TEDESCHI

I'm going to be 62 this year. I'm old, yet I feel so young. When I was a teenager, and someone said they were 60 years old, I thought they didn't know much of what was "really" happening; but they were the elders, and I believed they knew best. Old people were honored in my family.

All my grandparents were born in Italy and lived with their children in America. That was the way it was. Once I became conscious of my own evolution, I understood just how much these older generations and my extended family were my teachers.

Today everyone is scattered, and the young don't know the old; I see a kind of chaos, rapid change with no roots. Roots are important.

* * *

My father was the first-born male in an Italian family. He was a good student in school, and when World War II came, he joined the Marines. He was proud and full of respect for his country and respect for all people.

A tragedy occurred when he was 16 and his father died of pneumonia. The family had to give up their house because my grandmother, who worked in the sweatshops of New York, could not make ends meet. My father was a good athlete and was asked by the NY Giants to come to training camp. He had to decline this offer, even quit school, to go to work. He had one younger brother and two sisters, each looking up to him as the new father.

From these experiences my father came to balance his male and female energies. It was this balance in him that I loved so much. He was not the locker room macho guy, but a gentleman with integrity and compassion for his fellow man, nurturing to his family. He loved and respected his sisters and his mother whom we visited every Sunday as I was growing up.

My mother was only 5 when her father died of pneumonia, leaving 5 children to a mother who didn't speak English or have any marketable skills. The family had just bought their first house and the 4 older siblings went to work to feed themselves and keep the house. My mother became the beautiful princess in the family and remains in that role today. Her mothering skills were typical for a person who lived her culture and feared most things.

She left my father after 20 years of marriage. I was 14, and my sister was 17. My mother planned to have my father move out and our new father move in. Back in the 1960's there was little question that the children would stay with the mother. But my sister and I chose to stay with my father. Since he worked from 6 am to 8 pm, we were basically on our own to go to school, keep house and guide ourselves to adulthood. It was a learning opportunity that definitely shifted my consciousness and made me a strong doer in life. The male in me prevailed.

* * *

I lived predominantly in my mind as a male for the next 30 years. I went to college, advanced in my professional job, owned my own business, and made a salary of six figures. I was completely enrolled in the world of doing, acquiring, and partying.

I met a woman whom I felt was the true love of my life. She was beautiful, intelligent and fun. We loved and danced the nights away, and then one day, I came home from work, and she was gone. She left a note telling me she didn't love me anymore. I was devastated at the time and it was a real turning point in my life. I realize in hindsight, that my many past relationships were never really love. I had no idea what love was.

So where did I learn to love? Where did I find that energy to love again?

My Great Aunt Rose was the person who taught me that the most important thing in life is love. She was my father's Godmother. I met her late in life as she lived far away when I was younger. But later, quite coincidently, we lived in the same city. In 1983, before my father died, he visited me in Rochester and asked me to look after her once he passed on. I agreed and once a week after work, my partner and I would visit her. We got to know her and to love her.

When we arrived at Aunt Rose's home, the wine and cheese came out and the stories of the old days began. She was 97 at the time, lived alone, still cooked, cleaned and had all her faculties. She spoke with a heavy accent, and she loved everyone in her life. She had stories to tell about each one. At the end she would say, "I loved them so much," and she would cry at the happiness she remembered with them. She came to this country and was taken in by my great-grandmother, her aunt.

She told me stories of coming to America in the early 1900's. It took nineteen days by boat; everyone brought their own food on board and lived with many others downstairs in the hold. She told me of her first view of the Statue of Liberty, of how my great-grandmother bought her a coat to wear. She was 16 and came to America to make a home for her 3 brothers who worked. The routine was, work in America and send money home so more family can come. She lived down the street from my great-grandmother, and she would visit with her every day and they would drink their homemade wine. My great-grandmother had 8 children of her own, and a husband who didn't work. She was a wet nurse to orphan children to earn money for food for the family. The conditions were deplorable; yet living in the slums of Harlem, theirs was a family of love and happiness.

I began visiting my Aunt Rose daily towards the end of her life. She was the mother I never had at home. We laughed and talked and loved each other so much. I came to learn how much I was like my great-grandmother, how I had her sense of humor and her determination. I loved her too, and yet I had never met her. I finally knew though, what love really was. The male harshness dissolved in me, and the mother energy flourished from this point on in my life.

* * *

Over the years, from these roots, I have become a social activist. I have learned to spot love and passion in people, and when I see that, I try to nurture it and become a bearer of hope and inspiration to them. My activism is about leveling the playing field for everyone and encouraging each to reach her/his full potential. And, when the road gets rough, I advise people to look within for their daily strength. The trick is never to give up looking within until the goal is reached. Then, "Failure is Impossible."

So many of us take the easy way out and give up. We don't have the courage to persist. We get lazy or fall into victim mentality and pine away. If we can manage to stay balanced in our hearts, to be a mature male/female person, peace will come — no matter what happens.

In the past 12 months, I have had a series of tragedies and learning opportunities that have tested my strength, my faith and my agility to adapt. These are the challenges that have happened in my life over the past year.

I have watched my mentor and friend struggle through the effects of a serious stroke. My mother has become the victim of dementia with all the ramifications of that. We lost my 29-year-old nephew to suicide. My partner and I were in a horrendous car accident that left us both helpless in wheel chairs for several months. I sold my beloved family homestead and watched it get demolished.

I have watched my partner of 24 years go through brain tumor surgery and radiation treatments.

This was a stormy year, but I was able to stand firm and hold down the fort with my strong male energy, and to make our house a home with nurturance and care giving from my strong female energy. My role changes daily and easily. I have learned to surrender to what is and realize the obstacles are not opposing me, but are really rerouting me to where I am supposed to be.

I am simultaneously involved in many community projects. Every morning, I go within and ask one-line questions about the action I am to take that day. I receive answers, without exception. I tap into my Mother-Father energy, and go from being unsure of what to do, to certainty of action.

This is a gift we all have, if we can just learn to access it… to go inside and ask. This is where the answers live, in ourselves… in our Universal Selves… in our Mother-Father God within.

Marilyn Tedeschi is an urban educator, youth advocate, business entre-preneur and social activist whose interests lie in the economic development of the working poor. Marilyn is a co-founder of the Progressive Neighbor-

hood Federal Credit Union and the Community Micro-Enterprise Center. Marilyn is a graduate of SUNY Geneseo with advanced degrees in school administration. She is currently involved in development efforts for the Rochester Branch of the American Association of University Women and helping to develop the Women's Institute for Learning and Leadership in Seneca Falls, NY. marilyntee@aol.com

Aging and Writing:
Doors to the Next Dimension

BILLIE C. DELAWIE, PH.D.

As a Crone—defined by the ancients as "Wise Old Woman"—I look back at the terrain my journal has covered during the old paradigm now passing away, and I can see the trail of the Feminine as she has emerged in my consciousness.

For the most part, I am an Ordinary Woman living an ordinary life. I have three grown children and two grandchildren whom I love. Looking at me, clerks are sometimes patronizing toward the old woman they see; passersby kindly let me go first. I see and love them all as the emerging Feminine transforms the culture—and me—through humanity's evolutionary dance that began long ago.

There is also an Inner Child who has been ignored and abused, yet has refused to be broken. Composed of both male and female aspects, she has a story all her own. As both heroine and hero, she has led my Ordinary Woman beyond recovery into divinity.

In my journal, when I write what I hear and feel at the center of myself, the ego often arises through the voice of a Harsh Critical Judge. He threatens the Child with death and acts as if I were a Nazi war criminal: misplace a comma and he tortures me, again awakening the child's terror, paralyzing me.

This most often happens when I approach the source of my feminine creativity: my sexuality. Surprisingly, healing childhood sexual abuse has led me to spirit and I have become a willing conduit for other realities, readily available when I write. Yet when the Judge roars, the Inner Child's terror arises, and I cannot write. So I have learned to ease past ego's judgments, which are based in old worn out fears, and enter a new reality to reveal an improbable love story.

On daily walks, I used to pass beneath a huge palm tree whose fronds hung to the ground, providing shelter from passing cars. At the juncture of base and bark was a small ledge, wide enough to lean against, though not wide enough to sit on. Here I often perched on warm summer evenings, entranced by brilliant sunsets as the sun slid slowly beneath the Pacific. In winter, bundled in my blue parka and warm gray scarf, I would lean against the tree in the fog, watching the light fade until only street lamps shone through the mist, in a silence so intensely private that there was no other world.

It was on such an evening of fog and silence that I became aware of other presences, though no one else was about. I closed my eyes and slowly an image formed, as misty as the fog-enclosed streetlight: a wood-paneled tiered chamber - not large, but not small either. Men were seated in rows and were directing their attention toward me. Surely not, I thought, shaking my head to clear it; I'm imagining this.

Yet time is malleable, and the older I get the less rigid are the boundaries between these and other times. So I waited, and as the image clarified, I also began to hear voices, though I couldn't identify who was speaking. Somehow I knew that I was being challenged by a demand that I conform to cultural rules, and return to my place, a woman's place.

"No," I said aloud. "No, I won't do that. I have some significant purpose in being here. I have work to do."

There was a roar of laughter. Trembling with fear, my throat closed as I rose to face the old tree trunk. Opening my eyes, seeing the tree and hearing the laughter, I said again, "I have important work to do."

Sneering, jeering voices rolled over me. "I'll show you!" I responded through angry tears. "I'll show you."

In the years that followed, I returned often to the majestic old palm, taking my confused and aching heart there. Through intense loneliness, I wrestled with a multitude of powerful feelings, including shame and guilt for falling in love with a man not my husband. Divorcing my husband and giving him primary custody of our children disrupted everything the Ordinary Woman had been taught about womanhood. Yet within myself I knew that in responding to sexuality's call, I had responded to an energy even more powerful than that of motherhood —my own destiny

During these years, through inner and outer channels, sometimes startling information came to me. At the palm tree I learned that the men were the Council of Arimathea, a faintly familiar Biblical name. Through research I learned that Joseph of Arimathea had taken the chalice from which Jesus drank at the Last Supper and delivered it to England. The king gave Joseph the misty isle of Avalon on which he built Glastonbury Abbey, the first Christian church in England.

A fascinating story, I thought, but what was the Council of Arimathea, and what was its meaning in my life? Probably I was nuts. Such things don't happen to an Ordinary Woman like me.

Often I returned to the tree, perching on its base, wondering if the phenomenon would be repeated. Sometimes it was, and slowly the tenor of the meetings changed. One man stood with me, praising me for having left the conventional path for which I'd been trained. Tears still come to my eyes, my most reliable sign of authentic feeling, when I remember his staunch support.

To my surprise, even after moving half way across the city, the presence of Joseph of Arimathea came with me, leading me deeper into a spiritual life for which nothing in my Oklahoma past had prepared me. I remained skeptical about my sanity, and only shared my experiences in my writing groups where I felt very safe. Using runes, small tiles inscribed with ancient symbols, I integrated Joseph of Arimathea as representative of my own wounded inner Masculine aspect. Willingly he took on the many roles I assigned him: hero, lover, writing partner and friend, and, less willingly, villain, immature boy, wimp and rapist.

In my journal I wrote: "Banished from human consciousness eons ago, the Sacred Feminine suffered grievous wounds. She hovered within the subconscious of women and men, manifesting in dreams and intuition. During her absence, humanity evolved a patriarchal belief system that created our familiar material world. Existence with only a wounded Masculine, incomplete without the Feminine, has fostered inequality and injustice, and today threatens the survival of our planet and its inhabitants.

"I have in the past disrespected this hardworking male who's been denied so much of his authentic feelings. Now, the Sacred Feminine is returning through me, seeking union with the Sacred Masculine, facilitating the healing of both." Tears arose; sadness overwhelmed me as I realized that the frequent separations from my family were based in the separation of my own inner masculine and feminine; that falling in love outside my marriage had moved me to create a spiritual path that didn't exist until women like me co-created it—a Feminine spiritual path.

Through my tears, I heard Arimathea say, "I want you to give voice to my buried feelings, allow me to express my rage and grief without your buying into it. I need to be irrational, crazy, hurting sometimes, without your trying to fix me or shut me up. Witness the truth of who I am. I want to return to you after our eons-long separation."

He paused before he concluded, "I want you to love me and stand with me while I express feelings—in all their rawness and splendor—that I buried while I did what I had been trained to do, just as you did. Sometimes I feel angry, even violent. I'm afraid I'll hurt you. In my last life on earth, filled with loathing for the man I'd become, I was trained to use religion against women, to destroy their power. In reality I may be a poet, an artist, a writer or musician. A time may come when you will remember the man I was.

"I have a treasure for you that you can depend on. I can take care of you without having to pretend to be the warrior that I am not. Instead I am consort to the Feminine Herself. I don't want to go to war; I want to stay and make love with her, as I want to do with you.

"I am profoundly sorry to have driven you away from me. I want you to forgive me, that we may be reunited forever."

My heart broke open; tears flowed; eons disappeared.

Though he loved me from another dimension, we wrote and facilitated groups together for fifteen years from our different dimensions. In 2006 I recognized Joseph of Arimathea's energy in a former contemporary Catholic priest, relieved of his parish for his strong stand for women's ordination and his fierce inclusion of the Feminine aspect of God. Expressing his love for me in letters and unique drawings, he saw this Ordinary Woman as representative of the sacred Feminine herself, and a door opened for conscious partnership between the sacred Masculine and Feminine within me—a most precious gift of wholeness to the evolutionary Crone.

A pioneer in Feminine Spirituality, **Billie C. Delawie, Ph.D.** *has facilitated women's evolution through writing for 25 years. Her focus is on revealing women's authentic feelings and helping them release limiting patriarchal*

beliefs as they stand in their own authority. Author of Home is Where You Are and Crone Poet's Journal; Billie publishes a free monthly Croneworks Newsletter (http://www.croneworksnewsletter.com/newsletter.html).

Contact her at lovelycrone@sbcglobal.net or 619-276-6569

PART THREE

I Express My
True Self

STORY 18

The Light Within

KIM PRUCHA

Through the years, people have often said that they see a Light within me. These have been people I truly respect, people who are respected by others. I've wondered if they're crazy. The woman in the mirror has looked ordinary to me. I could see a few wrinkles, a few laugh lines, a few extra pounds...

But a Light? I just couldn't see it!

I wondered if everyone could see this Light. Why was I not seeing the Light they spoke of? That seemed to me to be the real question.

Focusing on the gray hair, the wrinkles, and the extra pounds made it difficult for me to see the real woman within. When I look at my kids, I see them as beams of light, glowing and inspiring me, bringing joy into my every day. I tell them they are beautiful and smart and amazing. I want them to see their own Light. I want them to know it's there and that others can see it and feel it.

But seeing my own Light hasn't come as easy.

I have done my share of inner work. I have read the books. I go to retreats and workshops and spend hours on the phone taking and facilitating teleclasses. My inbox is overflowing with spiritual literature. I can talk the talk, but have found "walking the walk" to be the real journey. Though I tell my children all the exquisite things I see in them, am I modeling something completely different?

What is this Light within me that people tell me they see? Is it God? Spirit? Universal Energy? Love? Peace? My search to know this Light has been a lifelong journey.

My family was not like that of my friends. I was born as a result of an affair that my mom had with a man who already had commitments to a wife and family. My mother was not living with—but not yet divorced from—an abusive, alcoholic husband with whom she had four children. My parents may have known, on some level that running off to Ohio from New York would not bring them what they needed. They ended up back in New York and separated before I was born, repairing old relationships and beginning anew.

After my birth, I lived with my maternal grandmother to allow my Mom to work the fluctuating hours of a waitress. I tell the story reluctantly, as a way of sharing a bit of my background, and who my parents were. I know that it is not a unique beginning, but rather one shared by many. I have a deep knowing that my parents loved me enough to serve as the vessels through which I came to be. Their love blessed me on a path of personal and spiritual searching and eventual healing.

How perfect for me! The gift my parents gave of not being physically present to me helped me put my search for Truth first. Without a "normal" family or the means to participate in activities or own things that my friends had, I turned instead to the love of my grandmother and to religion. Devoted to the Catholic Church, I seriously considered becoming a nun. I went to Mass every day for years, not because it was required, but because my Soul required a connection with Spirit and that was the only way I knew to reach for it. A humbling realization has been that each of these blessings has proven to be exactly what my soul came into this life to learn from and to shine through.

As a teenager, I attended a couple of weekend Catholic Youth Impact Retreats. I remember during the first of the small group sessions, we were asked to describe Christ. I listened quietly to the others at my table as they described a long-haired, robe-wearing, sandal-clad man...the typical image we have all seen in paintings and read about in descriptions. I struggled with what I knew my Truth to be and whether I had the courage to tell it. When my turn came, I shared what I was sure would upset the leader and would result in me being sent home.

I looked at each person in the circle and through tears, told them that I was looking at Jesus when I looked into their eyes. I felt somehow stronger, empowered even, because I told what was my Truth. I waited for the reaction. The only person who spoke was the 30-some year old woman who was leading our group. Through her own tears she told me that it was the most beautiful description of Jesus she had ever heard. We had an instant connection that lasted the rest of the weekend, and she shared her feelings when my mother arrived on Sunday to pick me up and take me home to my grandmother's house. Perhaps it was through my Truth-telling that a glimmer of Light began to emerge.

There have been times since then when this Light of inner confidence has shone through. Perhaps it was in the choice to breastfeed my babies and to educate and support other women wanting to do the same. Or was it in the decision to homeschool my kids? Whenever self-doubt crept in to ask, "Who do you think you are?" my Light weakened. I wondered if the Divine Light that had empowered me on that weekend long ago really only expressed itself through important, holy people and saints...not me.

When I was forty years old, I went through a time of questioning. I was homeschooling my three children and knew that was the path we should be on, yet there were questions. I had been happily married for thirteen years and very much in love with my husband, yet there were questions. I was involved with our church, going to Mass as expected, yet there were questions. What could possibly be going on?

It took some time and a lot of spiritual searching to discover what the questions even were. Naturally, until they presented themselves, I couldn't feel the power of my answers. It turned out that the questions centered on my spirituality. I was not living my Truth. I was living up to the expectations of the church and other people. I was not living up to my own expectations. I wasn't even sure what they were.

My quest became to remember who I was and where I was going. The most profound remembering came with the realization that I am One with Spirit. That deep knowing opened my heart and allowed me to take the steps needed to begin a new phase of my journey. After years of asking and answering questions of my self, it was time to step forth and begin to share with others.

Occasionally, I would receive e-mails from James Twyman, founder of The Beloved Community, telling about the Seminary of Spiritual Peacemaking. I resisted. I hit "delete." Another class would begin. Delete, again. Finally, one day it seemed that I couldn't say no anymore. It was time; time to say "Yes!" And I did.

The lessons and readings for the Seminary of Spiritual Peacemaking brought me to an entirely new level of discovery. Where once I saw limitations, I began to see possibilities. Where once lived doubts, there was now assurance. I could see that I was capable of moving beyond the fear and walking into the Light. It became clear to me that I had been in fear of the Light all along. I had chosen to live in the shadow instead of owning the Light. I finally came to know that my Truth is the Light.

Walking in the Light of my Truth continues to be a process for me. Opening to the growth of my soul brings a joy that I wish for everyone.

I have known the Light as a sliver of self-assurance and as a knowing that I've made the right choice. It has peeked through when I stand up and allow my voice to be heard. It is possibly most profound in the quiet knowing that as I stand in my Truth, I am choosing to Be Here Right Now as the beautiful Light that I am.

Now when people say they see a Light within me, I know exactly what they mean.

Kim Prucha is a Minister of Spiritual Peacemaking and Seminary Facilitator, walking the journey with new seminary students in The Beloved Community. She enjoys speaking with individuals and groups about Spiritual Peacemaking. Kim facilitates book study groups, workshops, retreats and tele-classes. Kim is a co-founder of The Peace Sisters, an organization creating cultural and educational events to foster a greater presence of Peace in our communities. She is also a Kundalini Reiki Master. Contact her at kimip99@aol.com

Coming Into My Conscious Voice

JOANNA CLARK

What is it to be an evolutionary woman and make conscious choices in self-expression?

Eleanor Roosevelt said: "In the long run, we shape our lives, and we shape ourselves. The process never ends until we die. And the choices we make are ultimately our own responsibility."

We are in a constant state of evolution. The exciting thing about being alive at this time is that we can be conscious of this and choose how we respond to events. We can drift with the current, letting ourselves be bounced around, or we can listen to our inner guidance and declare who we are.

My vision is that my inner self and outer expression are congruent. I am also in partnership with the outer environment, influenced by outer forces. I am in a dance with life! I choose my thoughts and words mindfully -- while being free and unafraid in my expression. It requires a two edged listening: within, to myself, and without, to others, being in tune and connecting. When I am in the flow, it works beautifully. It is a learning process, never ending; always a source of discovery, delight and disappointment all mixed together. It is a continuous journey of increasingly authentic, satisfying self-expression.

I recently attended a meeting of a group with the intention to be Spirit led. During that meeting, two people stood out by the way they expressed themselves. Joan was hard edged and single-mindedly bent on making her point. She was clearly determined to have her way. This was in sharp contrast to the demeanor of the rest of the attendees: calm, peaceful, listening, and open to discussing possibilities. She was out of touch with the rest of us, and seemed to be out of touch with herself. Mary, who had the task of guiding us, calmly kept bringing us back to listening to our hearts, to Spirit. She did not let the meeting be hijacked by the demands of one person, yet she was calm, loving and accepting of Joan, while gently and firmly keeping us to our stated purpose. I can empathize with Joan. I have been there, believing that I must make my point, that I must make them hear me. My vision is to be more like Mary.

FORMING AN INTENTION

Every year I set an intention for myself. This year my intention is to develop my voice. I started with a broad and rather vague declaration, letting it evolve from there. My first iteration was 'Finding My Voice.' I was aware of a sense of discomfort, of a gap between my perception of my presence in the world and the perception by others; a gap between what I voice in public and what I voice to myself. This gap has become narrower and narrower over the years. I used to dread being called on in class even when I knew the answers. Now I give workshops, teach dance and yoga and regularly speak to groups. My friends, family and coworkers see me as strong and assertive and very self-expressed. So why do I continue to perceive myself as unexpressed, awkward and tongue-tied? Perhaps my perception is outdated!

After living with 'Finding my Voice' for a bit, I realized that stating it that way implied that I did not have one, or did not know where it was, and reinforced the unease rather than easing it. I shifted to

'Using My Voice.' Almost immediately I had trouble in my voice box. Singing hurt and made me cough. I love to tell stories but talking too long makes my voice raspy, and my throat sore. The ENT doctor recommended a videostrobe camera session with a speech therapist. This revealed that I have been causing strain by trying too hard, using "false" vocal chords instead of my real vocal chords. Cosmic! I have been trying too hard, and using the wrong equipment. Now I am having sessions with a speech therapist. Wow...at 64, I am learning how to talk.

PHYSICAL AND METAPHYSICAL LEARNINGS

While I am learning new ways of using my physical voice, I am also learning about metaphysical voice through Visionbuilding [Visionbuilding is the creation of Margaret Shepherd, www.visionbuildersinstitute. com.] The lessons often parallel and reinforce each other. For example, it is important to have breath support for speaking and singing, so I am doing exercises that teach me conscious use of the breath. With Visionbuilding, I am learning to build metaphysical inner support; to listen to the guidance within, to trust my feelings and the connection that I have with Spirit. Inner support begins with me. If I do not respect my thoughts and feelings and give myself permission to speak, who will? There is a great deal of freedom in this shift from looking to others for permission to giving myself permission within. I am granting myself the authority to be me.

To reinforce listening to inner guidance, I am sitting in stillness at least once a day and doing activities that call to me. These include creative pursuits, yoga and reading books that inspire and edify me. Rather than fitting these in after my obligations, I schedule them first.

LEARNING WHEN TO TALK AND WHEN TO BE SILENT, OUT OF CHOICE, NOT INTIMIDATION

I am three months into this experiment, and I have had several instances where I have behaved differently. The common denominator is a growing inner freedom. I am letting go of outmoded beliefs about myself and 'them.' I am confronting and moving through fear of rejection, looking foolish, being wrong, etc. Less often do I look back and wish I had said such and such.

One instance occurred at a family gathering. In my family of origin, I am often quiet, as we have very different beliefs. Talk about politics or issues of the day can quickly turn into much yelling and little listening. At a recent gathering, I asked to have a civil dialogue about who everyone was thinking of voting for and no diatribes, please. It was a good discussion, heartfelt and very civil, none of the usual stuff. I got a little loud at one point and was called on it. We used that as a springboard to make an agreement about what could work for us in future discussions.

I like my progress in just three months. I have come into a new ease and freedom to just be myself. My own inhibitions--those responses learned earlier in life--have been the biggest barriers to being my vision. I have realized that I am a 'free spirit,' a unique non-linear being who does best living a life full of collaborative creative activities. I honor who I am first and from there find people to work and play with and places to flourish.

I accept who I am and who I am not. I prefer to be with those who accept me too, but I do not need special environments to be okay with myself. Sometimes I speak up, sometimes not. Sometimes I am brilliant, other times clumsy. I am a work in progress, learning as I go. I love my life. I am writing this book with 44 women, participating in a group oil painting show, integrally involved in the leadership of my spiritual community, enjoying my friends and family. It's great to be an evolutionary woman. I will keep developing my voice, and who knows what evolution will take place?

There is a crowd of daffodils getting ready to bloom outside the window. They are the only spot of color in that part of the yard. What if they were not there? What if they did not bloom? The loss might not be noticed by most. You and I are those flowers. We are unique expressions of life. There is no one like you in the entire world. Have the courage to express your unique self, and we all benefit. We each need to blossom as the person we are, to give life to our way of being in the world for its sake, for our sake, for all our sakes.

"There's a dream in you that is waiting to be born. You have a unique way of loving, of giving, of comforting others that the world around you desperately needs. There's a talent, a style, a promise that is etched into the deepest part of your soul, and is coming forth right now in a way you could never have imagined."
- REVEREND MICHAEL BECKWITH

Joanna Clark was born in Fargo, ND, and grew up all over the US and in Spain, courtesy of the US Air Force. Life experience includes: Coaching Creatives, teaching and performing Improvisational Dance, Myers-Briggs Type Indicator leader, designing workshops, teaching yoga, giving Contextual Bodywork sessions, dancing the Flamenco onstage in Madrid, riding in barrel races, Woodstock in '69. Married 42 years, three children, 2 grandchildren. Lives in Columbia, Md. Current explorations: conscious evolution,

artful journaling, painting, and writing. Coach University 2001. Bachelor Philosophy/Creativity and Movement. PSU 1982. Joanna can be reached at coachjoanna19@mac.com or web.me.com/coachjoanna19

One Page at a Time - Writings of an Evolutionary Woman

SAGE KNIGHT

Dear God -
I am going to write a chapter for "Conscious Choices - An Evolutionary Woman's Guide to Life". Please guide me, help me, make your presence known to me as I write. Please be with me. Thank you, God.
Love, Sage

a.m. - Taking my time. Feeling my feelings. This is a warrior's path for me today. I have been feeling what I would describe as anxiety – physical anxiety as opposed to worry. As though the very tangible essence of old memories have personality and are crying out to be heard, to get out, to be seen. As though maybe I've been acting okay about things that are not. Things I have been settling for, putting up with, will no longer be tolerated; the Universe Itself will no longer allow me to devalue Its precious daughter, Sage.

I had no idea that when I made a decision to turn my will and my life over to the care of God, I was actually erecting, finding, turning my life over to stronger boundaries. I surrendered my will, and found a stronger will. Who would have thought God's will for me would be so protective, so fierce, so alive and so dynamic? It was all that I never had from anyone as I was growing up.

At first, I was concerned that this anxiety was a weakness. What I am realizing, as I write this, is that it is simply the past fear, terror, panic and desolation expressing its way out of my body, out of my life. I am finally safe enough and strong enough and aware enough of my own value that it can all come up without killing me. I welcome this, and I am so grateful for the love and support and time that I can devote to my own healing, to my own path.

a.m. ~ Last night at dance, I was 'I Am' again. A Priestess, that is the word...or simply 'Woman', my favorite title. 'Woman' holds such power, love and beauty! So sensual am I as Woman! I truly love Woman as Sage...

I was drawn from the back of the room to the altar, through the flimsy veil of my self-consciousness to the candlelit stage and the feet of our leader for the night. I touched her altar objects, picked up the gourd; decided I could and I must hold it in my hands. No one else did this. Perhaps no one else is a temple priestess, born to walk barefoot to the council meetings, in charge of the ledgers and the land...

I knelt low and bowed deep, no feeling of submission at all, as I recognized my own form before me, a woman I could serve as I serve my own self, my own mother, daughter, or sister. How long has it been since I served the divine as woman...

As I turned back toward the room, caressing the wooden floor beneath my body, I could feel the life of the trees, the support of the earth, of the Mother; and I was strong, aware of my roots and my bones.

When I stood up to dance, my core was intact; my movements informed by this conscious contact with who I was, who I am, who I will always be.

And I am not alone.

There are many of us, sitting in circles, creating pockets of peace, weaving a prayer shawl with the threads of our stories, cultivating a resonant field of kindness and depth. Every thread is precious, unique and essential. Some are invisible, but their strength is felt all the same.

a.m. ~ I don't know how it happened, only what happened. This morning, God and I had a little dialogue. I'd felt so tender, so raw about what I would submit to the book. It's so important, I want it to be my Most Profound writing. I felt that old pressure to succeed, so I asked for help, for guidance with my writing. Here is what I heard:

"Your chapter is already acceptable in My eyes."

I haven't even begun writing yet, and I have acceptance from God Almighty! I know I have acceptance from the editors, they invited me. Where is the pressure coming from? Who's left to accept my work...?

I am.

I realized I expected myself to be uber human, super mom, wife, leader, writer, whatever. I have this crazy transparent belief that I am required to perform great things in order to take up space on the planet, or on the page. I can accept that for other women it's enough to be a part of the circle, but I have to get an A+, as always. I've paid dearly for this lie, in sleep, joy, intimacy and peace of mind. No more.

I got down on my knees and prayed in gratitude, joyously declaring my willingness to accept myself today. As I am.

How long and in how many life-pervasive ways have I been trying to be enough? I don't even want to know...I just want to soak in this warm, healing salve of acceptance, to let it soothe the aching muscles of my soul.

When I went on my morning hike, I felt a lightness of being in every step, saw beauty in every leaf...Today, I don't have to be special. I'm thrilled to be alive, to do my best and to be my own favorite.

a.m. ~ I did not sleep. I awoke around 2:30 and stayed awake until 6. It was hell. Nothing would induce sleep, not an orgasm, a protein drink, homeopathics or Shelley's magic Qi Gong technique. I was up for good.

Today's Actions:
1. Take care of myself.

That's all I'm willing to commit to today. Today I am taking care of Sage. I have some resistance, but I have even more allowance. If it were a child who'd not slept, I'd offer compassion and TLC. For cryin' out loud, I'm changing neuro pathways in my brain! I'd like to do this with love and kindness.

a.m. ~ Women with huevos ~ I am surrounded by them.

I guess a man with huevos is a man with balls, guts, a guy who can tough it out. But the literal translation of 'huevos' is not 'balls'. It's 'eggs'. That's pretty funny!

A woman with huevos has feminine guts: the courage to stop toughing it out and surrender to what she is birthing. This courage goes deep. It is a conscious choice to let go of control and open to new life.

I have been so deeply touched by these women with huevos who've chosen to birth this book. We show up for each other, for ourselves, and for this little anthology of kitchen table wisdom; our wisdom, our mothers' wisdom, the milk and blood and bones of women. Wise, beautiful women. And I am one of them. I am a woman with huevos.

When I said, 'yes', to writing a chapter, I was chosen for who I am, my story accepted before a word hit the page. With the power of unconditional acceptance, all Evolutionary Women were invited, welcomed into a resonant field of shared warmth and support, a literary water birth, with a focus on making each mother as comfortable as possible so she could deliver her precious gift to the world. I am totally transformed in this midwifery of kindness.

When someone is truly listening, my authentic voice finds its way quite naturally and often irrepressibly out of my body and into the world. It knows when it is and is not welcomed and will not waste life force in superficial, distracted or competitive environments.

As I sat on the author calls week after week, I felt the relief of sinking into a warm bath as all guards melted away and out came my most tender, raw, fierce, frightened and joyous feelings. This is the world I desire for my evolutionary daughter. And my evolutionary son.

a.m. ~ My chapter is due in two days. I've carved out today and tomorrow. I've decided my most authentic writing is my journal, so all that I have on my plate is to go over the last several days, type it up and send it in. The real work is done, and I can relax. I think I'll take a nap...

But first I want to declare ownership of my brand new Macintosh laptop. I'm a professional writer with a bi-weekly column on self-care, yet for over a year, I've been writing on the family PC amidst the chaos of my ten year old son's room. A typical workday begins with the removal of a half empty lemonade glass, a day old apple core and miscellaneous legos. Sometimes there is a path from door to desk, but not always.

I don't mind the mess. It's his room. What I mind is being in it. So, I've decided Mom's getting a Mac.

It will be all mine, a tangible symbol of respect and self-love, a testament to my work, my voice, my contribution. I will have my own portable writing office, whose door is emblazoned with the symbol of Eve: an apple with one bite missing. I will be joyously chewing that one bite...slowly...taking my time...feeling my feelings.

Sage Knight, ALSP, is an author, mentor and mother who walks on fire and births in water. She lives in Topanga with a beautiful man, their two children and several pets and leads monthly women's circles in the Los Angeles area, reminding mothers, daughters, sisters and friends to trust themselves and each other. Visit www.generationsofwomen.com and receive a free copy of her wise and silly Living Well column.

On Becoming a
Wild Wonder Woman

JAN ST. JOHN

For as long as I can remember I have wanted to fly. Maybe that's why I've always loved Wonder Woman. What would life be like if I had her kind of freedom ....and so many magical powers?

As a Catholic kid growing up (Archdiocese of Chicago, to be exact), I saw that the men had the power. It was the priests who changed bread and wine into the body and blood of Christ. Did I ever challenge that in my obedient Catholic girl mind? Never.

The magic began for me when I made the conscious choice to let go of all religions and embrace the One That Dwells Within. In my personal "magical, mystery tour," I said goodbye to the Catholic Church and hello to my "divine feminine."

It began when I was 12, when my mother brought home our first color TV (they had just come out), and I couldn't believe that Gary Moore and Carol Burnett could actually come into my living room and make me laugh out loud. After that first "Ah-ha," I started to see the awesome power of the mass media. What if I could actually produce my own shows...and put them on the air? Even at that early age, I could feel the stirrings of a "life purpose," a way to fly.

Armed eventually with a degree from Northwestern and a fiery passion for social change, I landed a job at NBC Chicago. It was all great except for one thing. There was no room for innovation or creative thinking...not with the advertisers calling the shots and the powers-that-be wanting to play it safe.

Guided from within, I decided to leave the corporate media world and do what any red-blooded American girl would do in the search for meaning: get married and start a family.

When the kids were small, I actually started a balloon delivery business. I became a full-fledged entrepreneur, delivering bouquets of helium balloons to homes, parties and hospitals where people really needed a "lift." It was a glorious ride and gave me my first taste of true independence. My Wonder Woman days were off to a great start!

The Big White Light went on when I met Barbara Marx Hubbard in 1984. It was my Great Awakening in terms of discovering my deeper life purpose. Barbara saw that my personal mission was part of the greater whole...and how my piece fit perfectly into the mosaic.

I interviewed Barbara on my radio show in Chicago when she was running for Vice President of the country on the Peace Room platform. Within days, I got an inner signal to sign up for this highly unique campaign. I had never been political, but I was clear that I was being "called to my post." I trusted that call and, consequently, helped sign up over 200 delegates to put Barbara's name in nomination for Vice President of the United States.

It was the year Geraldine Ferraro ran...and women's voices were being heard around the country...including mine.

My crusade to make some kind of difference in the world guided my every move, and I loved it. My soul had been yearning for meaning and purpose, and this was a real "crash course" in social transformation.

When I finally packed it up to move to California and join Barbara, the New Age Movement was in full force. There were workshops galore, ocean walks and first-time experiences at every turn. My life as a wild wonder woman was gaining steam!

The greatest challenge on this wild and wonderful journey has been keeping my head above water financially. Sometimes it feels like I'm swimming fearlessly through the waters of life… and other times it feels like I'm drowning. I remember Barbara saying, "Nobody pays you to do your vocation of destiny." It's true. Yet, somehow I've managed to survive…even thrive…in the most beautiful places on earth, like Santa Monica and Marin County, CA (where I currently reside with my wonderfully wise and devoted partner, MaxWell).

What did my soul desire to create? I knew I had a "vocation of destiny," and all I wanted was to go tell the story…for all the world to hear. Accordingly, I hosted talk shows on both public and commercial radio for nearly a decade. My joy was "inner-viewing" the emerging movers and shakers, everyone from Deepak Chopra and Marianne Williamson to the one and only Shirley MacLaine.

In those days, I called my work a "media ministry" and often had my collection basket out for much-needed contributions to the cause. I discovered the "secret" to having money is just creative ideas.

Following my dream to make a difference in the world of radio and television has seen me through the best and the worst of times. Once, when I was questioning my progress, I heard a voice. It said that God was not done with me yet. I had to complete my mission on earth…in the media. I had no idea what that would look like, but that faceless voice, my inner knowing was guiding my every move.

One of the highlights of my career was working on the movie set of "Swing," a feature film starring Jacqueline Bisset, Jonathan Winters and the late Nell Carter. It made me see how movies are like real life. We get to make the whole thing up, scene by scene.

Jackie played an angel who came back to earth as a wild wonder woman with platinum hair, wearing a sexy red dress. Her message in the movie: go for your dreams and don't let anyone stop you.

The whole experience inspired me to write my own screenplay

about the first American woman President. It was probably the most creative, liberating and exciting thing I have ever done. I've pitched it all over Hollywood and continue to feel the script is going to find a home, maybe even at Disney. The energy of the "divine feminine" is now emerging full force on the planet, so maybe Hollywood will come round. I do believe it is finally "our time and our turn."

Another important part of my journey to becoming a wild wonder woman has been embracing the path of the Goddess. Once in a special ritual, I danced to my favorite, spirit-filled music and shed my clothes while being witnessed by a small circle of sisters-in-the-light. It emancipated another aspect of my BEing and helped me free my feminine spirit.

This book, being co-created by evolutionary women, is also a very good sign-of-the-times. When women's voices fill the pages and take to the airwaves, we become an irresistible force in the world. I hope that all of the stories contained herein touch the lives of thousands, if not millions, of women seeking their own next turn on the evolutionary spiral.

Having faith in things unseen and trusting the process are the hallmarks of evolutionary women. We are models for doing what we love; knowing that all we need will be given. And, let's enjoy the journey!

My dear friend, LiLi, is founder of the Ministry of Fun. She has anointed thousands of ministers around the world with the following pledge: "If it's not fun, don't do it. If you must do it, make it fun. Each of us has a one to one connection to the ONE."

Now I am entering a new phase in my personal evolution. Jane Fonda claims that when women turn 60, they are beginning Act 3 in their lives. As a media person, I love the idea of life as a stage play. Now, it seems, the curtain is rising one more time. I only wish I knew all my lines...and how it all ends. But that would take the fun out of it, don't you think?

Mostly, these days, I let the Universe handle the details of life. It's way easier on the nervous system and generally more effective than shaking the tree before the fruit is ready to drop. Now I am letting the fruit fall when they're ripe, picking them up when I feel like it.

Am I crazy to live like this? My oh-so-practical sister in Chicago might think so. Yet, she also sees that my life is flowing, filled with good things and good people. Her 3rd Act looks very different from mine, yet her story is playing out exactly the way she wants it, including her own wonderful cast of characters.

My strong recommendation is that once you discover your creative bent, follow it. See where it leads you. Have fun along the way and measure your success by the joy you experience on the journey. Ideas for funding, people to call and connections to make will flow to you when creativity is high.

Write your novel. Sing your song. Start a ministry of your own. Do whatever turns you on...with an open heart and mind. Then, see. What does the Universe want to provide? What are you magnetizing as a result of sharing your most creative and best Self? Put the Law of Attraction to work for yourself and join the ranks of other wild wonder women. It's one great ride!

Jan St. John *has a passion for positive media and a deep interest in the "divine feminine." After a long career hosting and producing radio shows (from "Women of Courage" to "Breakthroughs – News for a Positive Future"), Jan mostly likes to write these days. Her favorite genre is screen-writing, and she's now creating a series of short stories for children with one primary theme: Be Love and Enjoy the Journey. She dedicates this chapter to her daughter, Emily, and granddaughter, Emma.*

From Emergency to Emergence:
Going from Survival Mode to Living
An Authentic Heart-Centered Life

DEBORAH KOPPEL MITCHELL

"As human beings, our greatness lies not so much in being able to remake the world - that is the myth of the atomic age - as in being able to remake ourselves."
- MAHATMA GANDHI

There comes a time when the need to redefine some of the meanings we have attached to words, thoughts and ideas that we've been holding as truth becomes necessary if we are to progress in our human development. We also must be willing to look at what is not working for us, and to let that go!

At this mid-point of my life, as I am in my fifties, I am reassessing the ways in which I have been functioning and defining my Self. There is much that no longer works for me in a positive way.

I recently got hit with a "bug," some type of bacterial infection that had me down for four weeks. During this time I found myself having to reexamine many of the ideas I have around my self worth.

In my normal, everyday life I am very busy keeping up with things--things that don't get done unless I do them. I generally take care of these things with feelings of joy and gratitude. I get a sense of worth and usefulness. During this "down-time" of being ill and physically unable to do all that I do, I discovered that I was experiencing feelings of worthlessness, and many valuable revelations began to surface.

I found myself questioning my very identity. "Who am I," I asked myself, "when I can't keep juggling all the plates I have going? What if I stopped everything and no longer pressured myself with keeping my business going? Who am I without it?" I even found myself wondering why my husband would want to be with me if I can't keep it all going. Then I wondered how long had I been placing my value and identity on what I do rather than whom I truly am.

In Eckhart Tolle's book, *A New Earth: Awakening to Your Life's Purpose*, he conveys how "In normal everyday usage, 'I' embodies the primordial error, a misperception of who you are, an illusory sense of identity." This illusory sense of self stems from our ego.

After reading this, I had to ask myself when my ego had taken over so much of how I perceive who I am. And even more so, "Who am I really?"

A dear friend once described the essence of who I am by saying: "Deborah gives you a break." I know that being patient, loving and nurturing has been my natural way of being towards others. Why did I allow all that good stuff to get covered up when I related to my Self?

My husband and I made a big move from Los Angeles to Santa Fe in 2005. I thought this would be the big change that would get us off the treadmill of thinking we always had to be doing to be productive--to be successful. All the doing didn't allow for much being. It seemed that we were continuously working just to stay afloat. Fear had become much of the driving force beneath our existence. We were functioning from that core, gut survival area. We got a big nudge from the Universe to slow down and get in touch with operating from the heart.

Going from sea level to 7,000 feet alone was a huge adjustment, in which we literally, physically had to slow down. Nature envelops you here in Santa Fe. There is an acclimating to its rhythms that happens organically, and the cellular memory in which we are related to Nature is reignited.

What I hadn't realized was that my old norm of doing to feel I have value and purpose was a well-exercised muscle that was also naturally kicking-in, regardless of where we lived. I became hypercritical of myself when I didn't seem to be getting enough done, or if I felt like I needed to take a nap. It seemed I needed to create an illness in order to give myself permission to take a break.

The other day I got an inner nudge to go out on our land and simply sit in what I call my "Circle of Trees." I knew taking time to be in Nature would get me centered. This is where I get a sense of my Self--the Self that I am without doing. I find peace here. Here, I give myself a break. I feel this same peacefulness when I sit in the sacred environment of the Circle Gatherings I have been facilitating for so many years. Through this work, which I love, I create a sanctuary for all who participate—and for my Self. Our centering and wellbeing comes with doing that which naturally brings us joy.

Through all this self-exploration, I have come to realize that the state of "Being" is the muscle we want to exercise so that it eventually becomes our norm. In fact, once the state of Being becomes our natural way of functioning, we find our Selves being more present with all that we do. We become a human being fully Being. This is a process that takes practice, time and patience. I know I need to get my Self in a centered state of beingness to Be able to quiet the critical ego voice--to hear and follow my inner guidance.

The following are some exercises I found work for strengthening the Being Muscle:

- Take time to sit in Nature. Even if it is for a brief amount of time—though the longer and more open your schedule, the better. It is especially beneficial if you can actually sit on the earth. Simply breathe and allow your Self to be an observer with your eyes open or closed. Sit or lay back and watch the clouds--for hours at a time if you are able. Watch a sunrise or sunset. Listen to the rain, or flowing water. Just be.

- Rest. Give yourself permission to rest. Learn to tap into your body and spirit and honor the need for rest. If you feel you don't have time for an actual nap or break, at least give your Self the space to lie somewhere, flat on your back, and close your eyes and take ten deep breaths. When I lived in the bustling city and always seemed to be on a tight schedule—I would actually take time to pull over my car where I could safely park and recline the seat back and close my eyes for a few minutes, while taking slow, deep breaths. Get enough sleep at night. Eight hours is the preference. Figure out what is best for you.

- Do something in which you can lose your sense of Self and in which you can totally lose track of time. Art of any kind is especially great for this, as well as gardening or cooking--even cleaning or organizing. Your main focus is being fully present in the moment of whatever you are doing.

- Create and be in a sacred space. Lighting a candle can set the tone for a sacred environment immediately. This can be a place you have just for you or for special gatherings, such as a Women's Circle. This can also be experienced by simply sitting silently with a person or persons you love or are comfortable with.

- Give your self the gift of silence. For example, when you are driving in your car, let this be a quiet space. Create a meditation practice to be part of your routine. Give your head, your eyes, and your ears a break.

• Travel. Experience your Self somewhere you don't have any of the trappings of your everyday life. Just be out in the world.

The more we exercise this "Being Muscle," the more functioning from our heart-center becomes our norm, which allows us to create a positive environment for all. We step out of "survival-mode" into the thriving realm of unlimited possibilities. From here our true selves, our true paths, unfold before us naturally and in perfect time.

I am learning to trust this process and fully embrace my Self. This way of being allows me to evolve and emerge into an even more authentic, loving Human Being. I look forward to this emergence along with you and all of humanity.

Deborah Koppel Mitchell is a Circle Facilitator and publisher of Spheres Circles Magazine and website. Deborah is a contributing author of Inspiration to Realization and author of the upcoming series, Notes from a Modern Day Pollyanna. She is also creator of the "Pollyanna Power" product line she started developing in September, 2007. Deborah is available as a facilitator, consultant and for interviews. E-mail:spherescircles@earthlink.net

Visit www.sphereswomenscircles.com - To subscribe and to receive announcements from Spheres Circles and the free E-zine, Tools and Inspirations, sign up on the website.

STORY 23

Healing from Within:
A Midlife Transformation

KRYTA DEERE

"I have bad news, and I have good news" the man in the white coat sitting across the desk from me said in a soothing voice. I was his first appointment this July morning of 2002.

"You have cancer of the womb" he continued, "and I have arranged for you to have a complete hysterectomy."

My head started to spin. Only a few short weeks ago I had come in for a consultation because of spot bleeding and had a biopsy performed. Of course, there was always the nagging possibility in the back of my mind that the results could be positive. But hearing those words from the gynecologist seemed like a death sentence.

"The good news is that you can still have an orgasm," he added with a reassuring smile and confided that many of his patients told him that after the surgery they were able to enjoy sex for the first time in their married lives.

I was dumbstruck.

"You still have sex?" he asked probingly.

At age 61, sex was not foremost on my mind. And a hysterectomy in exchange for an orgasm seemed like a poor trade. I had just ended a dead-end relationship because it had not progressed beyond food, drink and sex. There were so many things I wanted to do in the Second Half of my Life and time was running short!

"What about diet and supplements, a change in lifestyle?" I asked hopefully.

The aging man in the white coat shook his head. "That won't help," he answered. "Sometimes we treat it with hormones, but you are too old for that. And in any case, your womb is no longer of use, you are no longer productive."

So this was it. This was the message: a woman is only of use as a pro-creator or as a sex object, to be discarded when she is no longer desirable or productive. Yet, this was the unspoken contract I had abided by all my life.

From an early age I was conditioned to give my power away to the Big Men in my life--to my father, who had punished me severely after having found out that I had played "doctor" with my friends and cousins, to my husband and lovers who had left me when I dared to show signs of my own creative willpower and strength. I had spent most of my adult life playing a game for which men set the rules. I had suppressed my femininity, trying to become one of "them." I was never comfortable in the role of mother, wife and lover. I was never in my female body! I had never learned what it means to be a woman, to be soft and vulnerable, attributes I had deplored as signs of weakness. My survival depended on my strength.

Until, one day, life offered me a chance to reconnect and become whole.

The process was slow and painful. It began in 1992, well before my diagnosis, when the rug of my miscreated reality and material existence was pulled from under me. I tumbled into the proverbial "Dark Night of the Soul."

I was in my early fifties then and started to ask myself the existential questions: Who am I? What is my Purpose in Life? What is the meaning of all of this?

Unable to deal with life, I fled into spirituality and to the safety of my log cabin in the mountains, reminiscent of my childhood in the Austrian Alps.

Except for the brief episode of my last excessive relationship, I lost connection to my roots and creativity. I lost the joy of being alive. I forgot how to play. Life was just too hard to deal with and had made me systematically shut down all my chakras.

And now the womb, the symbol of my femininity, was to be removed, discarded like a piece of garbage. My creative life-blood was trickling out of me, as useless as I had become in the eyes of Patriarchy. A woman's uterus is a place where emotions and memories are stored. For the first time ever I associated my reproductive organ with my identity as a woman, as a creator and a nurturer.

I remember sitting in the garden, swimming endless laps in the pool, looking at my flowers, observing their cycles of budding, blooming and fading. This was my life cycle as well. Friends told me that I needed to let go of the Old in order to start the New. Others stopped calling altogether, embarrassed by my condition. One of my close male friends responded to my news with "Gee, I am really sorry to hear that you have cancer. Now you just take good care of yourself." I never heard from him again. I had suddenly become "socially unacceptable." Leper-like.

Amidst all the fear and terror of the unknown, waiting for the surgeon's call, a small voice spoke to me, "What exactly are you afraid of? The worst thing that can happen is that you die. This you will do in any case. But as long as you are not aware of what caused it, what is at the root of all of that, you can have yourself cut up piece by piece, and you will never get well!"

It was as if the Universe was supporting this. During the next few days acquaintances in the Holistic Community started calling, inquiring about my health, offering assistance.

Convinced by them of the possibility of successful alternative treatments, I cancelled the surgery and focused on the healing power of the mind. I started doing visualizations, imagining troupes of Pac-men gobbling up cancer cells. Maintaining Faith and Trust in times like this was not always easy. Having chosen to go the alternative route, I had chosen to do it in secrecy, afraid of repercussions from the medical establishment. And then there was always the doubt of its effectiveness.

I spent the next two years doing exactly what the gynecologist told me was useless: detoxifying, changing my diet, my lifestyle, reducing my stress levels, engaging in extensive self-analysis, taking multi-doses of minerals and vitamins, having lymphatic drainage and meridian stimulation by vibrational machines, watching my pH/acidity balance--in short, taking care of myself. Walking, resting, sleeping a lot. It was during the small hours of the night when I became engaged in dialogue with my soul: I started to have intensive dreams, re-living many painful memories of the past, eventually leading to resolution. Always there was a feeling of urgency, of time running out. For the first time in my life I permitted myself to become really angry with people and situations I had allowed to happen.

Six months after the diagnosis I noticed a subtle switch: I felt the need to connect with God, to take refuge in solitude in order to let my new belief system take root. I felt vulnerable. I experienced a desire to live in the NOW, to connect with the new-found Self in me that wanted to express itself without the influence or demands from the Inner Child, Ego or Parent. I had matured. I started clearing out stuff, uncluttered my life and made patchwork quilts from the remnants of the fabrics of my past.

I felt as if I had died and been reborn. It became clear to me that I had realized most of my dreams, experienced joy and pain and learned from it. I was grateful for everything that had happened to me. I became aware that I was in the middle of a major transformation and that things to come will have to come from within, not from without.

I was ready to welcome life again. I felt the strength welling up in me, a strength that comes only if one is able to see oneself as whole in Body, Mind and Spirit, believing in one's immortal soul and not depending on the approval of others. I wrote in my journals: "When I detach myself I witness the Ego, running everything and everyone. My heart is welling up with love; I am able to let God take over, let everyone lead their own lives… I want to become a Wise Old Woman… I am embarking on a wondrous trip – the last stage to heaven, the highest peak."

Two and a half years after the diagnosis I was declared cancer-free. In September of 2007, at age 66, I graduated from the Natural Health Consultant's Institute in Montreal with a Certificate in Spiritual Psychotherapy. There I also studied Nutrition, Herbology, and Vibrational Medicine. I earned a second degree in Reiki. As my heart-space opened, so did my original refuge in the log cabin expand. I have converted my 12 acre property into a Holistic Wellness Retreat Center where I hope to help other women recognize the healing potential of Body, Mind and Spirit and to evolve to become Conscious Co-Creators.

Kryta Deere was born in Vienna, where she trained in Hotel Management. At age 18, she married and immigrated to Canada. There she embarked on a successful career in International Broadcasting, followed by Interior Design. An extended mid-life and subsequent health crisis were the catalysts for her deep interest in Psychology, Metaphysics and Alternative Medicine. She is a certified Spiritual Psychotherapist and owner of a Holistic Wellness Retreat Center in Morin Heights, Quebec.

www.krytadeere.com, contact@krytadeere.com, 450-226-3419

Walking Through the Fire: Facing Our Fears

ELEANOR LECAIN

On a recent trip to Ecuador, a friend brought me to a magical spring where we were surrounded by vibrant green leaves and singing birds. There in the Andes Mountains she told me, "I received a message in meditation three times to tell you, 'It is your destiny to speak and write, and now is the time.'"

The message hit me like a splash of cold water on my face – startling but refreshing. Deep inside, I knew what she said was true. But immediately, concerns and doubts surfaced. These were the fears that had surfaced every time I considered doing more speaking.

But this time, instead of listening to the fears and letting them stop me, I decided to face them head on. I would name the fears, and then re-frame them. My friend was very supportive, and described a similar experience she had been through recently. She told me her story: "I thought I was very courageous until a friend asked me, what are you afraid of? When I identified my fears, I reframed them and moved beyond them, and felt free."

So I went deep inside to see if I could name the fears. They were old friends by now, so I knew them well. I will share them with you here, in case you find it helpful in naming and reframing your own fears.

The first fear surfaced: "I've tried before to earn a living as a speaker, and it didn't work."

Then inside me was another voice, allowing me to reframe this fear: "The time was not right before. The time is right now. People are ready now to hear your message."

I started to cry. It had been so frustrating, but now, somehow I was facing the secret silencers inside, embracing them and reframing them.

That felt good! On to the second fear: "I am afraid that if I speak, I will be killed." Not surprising, really, given that when I was growing up, I saw President John F. Kennedy assassinated, then Martin Luther King, Jr, then Bobby Kennedy. Then there is the history of outspoken women being burned at the stake for 8 generations during the Burning Times.

The Reframe: "I would rather die speaking than live with my music locked inside. And I probably won't be killed since I have protection when I speak." (Also, my friend offered a session with someone who could help me process this fear and see what my life as a speaker could be like.)

Fear #3: "I am afraid I will not be able to earn money as a speaker, and I will impoverish my family if I try."

Reframe: It was as if the voice of Jesus Christ himself spoke, saying, "How can you worry about your livelihood? I would not let the hair of a sparrow be harmed. How much more protection will I give you, a daughter in service to the Lord!" My friend asked if I could get a line of credit to carry me until I earned money speaking. "Funny you should ask," I replied. "I just started getting into real estate investment and got a credit line increased to $45,000 just by asking. I don't want to use it, but it's there if I need it."

Tears were streaming down my face. This was big!

Fear #4: "I don't have anything significant to say."

Reframe: Another voice inside said, "Get out of the way. Let the spirit move through you. Be a channel, let the spirit flow." My friend told me that someone she knew had heard me speak and he said I was spectacular.

The fears kept coming.

Fear #5: "I know how to speak well, but I don't know how to turn it into a business so I can sustain myself."

Reframe: Now the other voice was actually laughing! "I have the best people in the world on speaking, publishing and marketing eager to mentor me! I am a member of the Enlightened Wealth Institute headed by Mark Victor Hansen, author of *Chicken Soup for the Soul*, the most successful book series ever sold (over 100 million copies!), and he has brought together a team of people to help me and others be successful authors. I have other resources on being a speaker just sitting on my shelf!"

Now I was actually looking forward to discovering the fears. Bring them on!

Fear #6: "I'm not sure what my message is." Since this struck me as another version of #4, I figured if it showed up twice it's really important.

Reframe: "Here's my message: We are living at the most extraordinary time in human history. The way through all our challenges is to live in harmony with each other and the Earth." We are moving from the Industrial Revolution to Living Systems, changing the way we think about ourselves and the world around us.

Fear #7: "I have lived in two worlds, 1) the world of politics and government, and 2) my spiritual journey. If I talk about my spiritual journey, people in government will dismiss me. I remember a colleague in the State House dismissing another woman by saying, 'Forget about her, she's gone spiritual.'"

Reframe: It's too funny I have this fear because the Right talks about Spirit all the time, and the Left is desperately looking for progressives who can bridge the God gulf with voters! By being mindful of the language I use, I can diminish ridicule and speak to that deep place in all of us. "I can weave political and spiritual understanding in my message. People are hungry for hope and inspiration, for spiritual understanding and nourishment."

Fear #8: "I am too old. My time has passed."

Reframe: "NOW is the time! All my experiences have deepened my understanding and prepared me to speak my truth with clarity and passion."

So now I am ready to pursue a life with more speaking and writing. Whenever one of these fears surface, I will remind myself of the Reframing I did around it. I hope you can do the same Naming and Reframing of Fears for yourself. Let's not let anything hold us back! The world needs us to be our highest and best now.

Of course, the invitation to write this chapter came at this time. When I meditated on what message to share with you, here is what came:

Speak to the women so they do not feel alone, so they know they are not crazy.

There are many women playing out the lives their parents want them to live. They are living goddesses trying to fit into society as it is.

They are afraid of speaking their truth because they fear they will lose their husbands, their connection to their family, the respect of their neighbors.

So they don't speak the spiritual truth they know. They hide under cover of social respectability.

But in their hearts they know there is a better way. They know we are spiritual beings. They know we should not be destroying Mother Earth.

"But what can I do about it?" they wonder. "The problems are so big, and I am so small."

Better to take one small step in the right direction then to run 100 miles in the wrong direction.

Now is the time to speak our truth. This time we will not be burned at the stake. We will be part of an historic shift to reclaim the Feminine and rebalance our world.

*Through speaking, writing and consulting, **Eleanor LeCain** explores how we can move forward from our current crises by increasing spiritual awareness and building on breakthrough solutions. Speaking worldwide and published from the New York Times to Le Monde, she authored Breakthrough! Innovations that Can Improve Your Life and Change the World, introduction by the Dalai Lama. She served as Assistant Secretary of State and director of futures planning for Massachusetts. A graduate of Yale and Boalt Law, she heads the WorldInnovationNetwork.org in Washington, DC.*

In Love with the Invisible

STAR RIPARETTI

FOLLOWING DELIGHT

I've said for a long time that my internal meter for my guidance is the Joy factor. If I feel an urge to go to the Sahara Desert and for some reason that sounds like fun, I will go and the means to do it will appear. On the other hand, if I think I have a message to go to a tropical island and for some reason at that moment it sounds more like work than fun, I take that as a sign and usually don't go. I choose win/win. Follow guidance, have fun. Since I'm not always sure if it is higher guidance or ego, I for sure want it to be at least half win/win-and that would be the fun part.

MY JOURNEY FROM ISOTOPES TO ESSENCES OF FLOWERS

It has been my pleasure to work with things you can't see or hear or touch or taste or smell. I was the chief technologist and director of the school of Nuclear Medicine at the Cancer Foundation in Santa Barbara, Ca. I worked with radioactive isotopes, each with their own vibrational frequency. Now as a producer of flower and gemstone essences I use vibrational frequencies at the other end of the spectrum. Both activities are equal in power, the latter in a much subtler, lighter and more graceful way. The substances I work with are still invisible, and blessedly without side effects.

I loved my job at the Cancer Foundation, I felt like I was doing a really good thing. I had a great title, and made a living wage. We would save people from exploratory surgery using diagnostic examination by tracing organs with radioactive material by giving isotopes that were specific for particular organs and then measuring and scanning and photographing where they went. We could see what was happening without having to cut people open.

I loved the job every day until the day I didn't. I remember a turning point sometime in the 80's. I was at the hospital one evening and I happened to run into one of the doctors I worked with. He asked me what I was doing there so late. I told him I was going to an acupuncture talk, and he told me not to waste my time. That comment was the gift. It was then that I realized that it was time for me to do something else. My friends and colleagues thought I was pretty crazy to leave such a "good job for a woman."

At first I began working half-time at the Cancer Foundation. Soon even that became uncomfortable when I realized that I was enjoying my time much more when I wasn't there. This had never been the case before. I remembered, "follow the fun factor", so I left the secure job and began my quest for my next phase of life. I began to study everything that had to do with plant medicine such as herbs and aromatherapy. Then one day, I saw the tiny ad that said "Flowers for Healing". That one line triggered me in a huge way and I began studying flower essences.

PERU CALLS

I took my first trip to Peru in 1988, while hiking the Incal Trail. I heard the message to make the Andean Orchid Flower Essence. I thought there was one. I didn't do anything about that message that kept repeating in my head for several years. I kept thinking that I wouldn't make a flower essence in Peru unless I did it with a Peruvian. Through a bunch of magical synchronicities I connected with a beautiful Peruvian man whose hobby is Orchids. This "connection" was the start of my business. At the age of 49, right after my last period and the beginning of menopause and entering the next stage of life as a crone, I created the first 7 Orchid essences. I could always talk to plants. It was then I began to hear them.

STILL IN SEARCH OF THE JOY FACTOR

It is my feeling that the power of Nature is the most important element that we have going. Working as a team with Nature is most rewarding; providing a high degree of satisfaction, a high happiness factor, and a beautiful sense of accomplishment. This partnership is nice for Nature and nice for the planet.

The garden feels like a place where we have the opportunity to play the Gods that we are. When we plant we are the arms and legs of Nature. We can take tiny seeds and choose where to put them to make the most amazing gardens. We can co-create with Nature fruits and vegetables that will sustain us and beautify our environment. And the newest experiment that I would urge everyone to try is, planting a seed that you have held in your mouth for nine minutes giving it the opportunity to learn your codes. Thus when it grows with your nurturing love, it will grow providing you what you need in order to heal. I read about this experiment in the most amazing books I have read to date, the *Ringing Cedars Series*, eight books that are translated from Russian. Nearly everyone I mention this practice to resonates with it.   It will be fun to see the results of these experiments. In these books Anastasia says the place we will find that peace is in our space of Love, in our own garden.

AND WHAT NOW– THE LAND IS MY LOVER

I bought twenty acres of raw, and I do mean raw, land in the foothills of Santa Barbara. When I am walking in mud nearly to my knees, when I'm looking at my yurt flattened and collapsed by the 100 mph wind, when I am looking at water spouting into the sky through a broken pipe, when I spill the diesel fuel for the tractor in my car, when I am cutting poison oak with 2 and 3 inch trunks, I'm asking "20 acres or a condo?"

The answer comes in a feeling. The feeling I get when I approach the land, my lover, to see what surprises – what gifts await. Will the Miners Lettuce be there today for a salad with Nasturtiums? Will I eat Strawberry Guavas from the bush during a rainstorm? Will I get to lick the pollen from the wild flowers?

Everything has a frequency, a vibrational rate of speed. Keeping these vibrations high is a precursor to good health. There are so many ways to do this. Healthy food grown with love on land that you love and nurture is a big one. When I am happy I serve the universe better. When I stay healthy I have more to give.

FOLLOWING THE BLISS REALLY IS THE ANSWER

In the *Ringing Cedars Series*, Anastasia suggests that everyone be given some land. She suggests one hectare, about 2 ½ acres, where one can grow their own food for their family. They can still have their city life if they choose, but the land cannot be sold, only passed on. They can have the land as long as they improve it by planting and growing organic foods and beautifying the land.

The food they grow isn't taxed and they can sell what they don't use themselves.

Wouldn't we all rather have food that was grown with love and affection rather than food grown with machines and chemicals and no love? Anastasia describes the vision in eight pleasantly compelling easy to read books that cover every reason you can imagine why it will work, and save the planet.

Now at this stage of our evolution it feels like we don't have the luxury of taking years to find our passion, our purpose. Use your feelings and desires as nudges before they turn to full blown pushes off the edge, to follow the things you are most passionate about. Allow your "joy factor" to be your guide.

GRATITUDE

Personally, I call myself an energy junkie. I go in search of the high vibes. For me those high vibes have come from raw food diet, lots of vibrational essences, Sai Maa, conscious languaging, Nature always, and most especially, like-minded friends. I think about where I would be had I made different choices, meaning retirement, 401K's, a life of certain economic stability, having a house nearly paid off (rather than a new 40 year loan at the age of 63). I wouldn't trade any of that for my fabulous experiences all over the world out on my edges, always poised to fly following my internal joy meter…and being grateful for the grace.

Star Riparetti is an Aquarian visionary who was born and resides in Santa Barbara, California. She is the founder of Star Essence, which produces Flower and Gemstone Essences. Star speaks nationally and internationally

and has been on radio and TV. Star is a partner in a new paradigm venture with indigenous people in the high mountains of the Andes, as well as tending to the love of her life, 20 acres in the Santa Barbara foothills.

312 W. Yanonali Street Santa Barbara, Ca 93101

phone/fax 805-965-1619
toll free 888-277-4955

www.staressence.com   www.andeanlodges.com   bliss@staressence.com

The Goldilocks Code: Getting Life Just Right

KIMBERLY MAROONEY

Five exciting weeks in Europe! I had the trip of a lifetime working my way through England, Holland, Germany and Slovenia. The most wonderful, loving and generous people came to see me everywhere I went. In Germany, 1500 people heard me speak at the Angel Congress. Afterward, hundreds of people waited in line for hours to tell me their stories. For the next two days, we wept tears of healing and love as we embraced in deep soul connections while an impressive lineup of international angel experts took their turns on the stage. This was most certainly a highlight of my professional life.

Happily tired when I returned home, I thought a week of rest should do it. That stretched into a month, then two. I had to cancel events and couldn't schedule anything new. I couldn't think. Six months passed in this dull fog, resulting in financial disaster.

As I recover, I am facing a major pivotal moment in my life. At the top of the list is the question, "How am I going to support myself financially?" I'm unable to do what I was doing before. So here I am at 50-something asking myself the question, "Who do I want to be when I grow up - again?"

At first I was terrified and felt confused which triggered feelings of failure. But I didn't take that road. Instead, I chose to see the opportunity.

THE POWER OF CHOICE

Every choice we make, no matter how small, either takes us closer to our true being and our soul's calling, or leads us further away. We all make many choices every day without realizing that each little choice we make has a cumulative impact.

I've made many choices over the last year. Some have resulted in a lovingly supportive group of friends who inspire the best in me. Other choices have become counterproductive, taking me away from earning money. Add in health challenges that make me feel helpless, and I clearly need to re-evaluate and change.

My cash flow quandary is a wake up call from my soul inviting me to stop and listen within. If I don't take the time to know myself, how can I possibly make good choices that will lead to a satisfying life of purpose and financial balance?

Sound familiar? Are you in a similar state of change? I pray that my journey will help you with yours.

THE GOLDILOCKS STORY

This brings us to the story of Goldilocks. One day she was walking through the woods when she came upon a house. Curious, she looked in the window and saw three bowls of steaming porridge on the table. Her tummy rumbling with hunger from the aroma of the porridge, she tried the door. It was unlocked, so she excitedly let herself in.

First she tasted the porridge in the great big bowl with a great big spoon, but it was too hot! Burning her mouth, she dropped the spoon and stepped away. Next, Goldilocks took a bite from the middle-sized bowl and yuck - it was too cold. With disgust, she put the middle-sized spoon down. Last, she tried the porridge in the wee little bowl.

It was "just right," so she ate it all up!

While there is more to this story, the relevant part is "not too this, not too that, but just right." This brings us to the main point:

How do we know what is just right for us when we don't know what "just right" is?

This is the key dilemma when we make decisions, isn't it? How do we know what we really want? Most of our choices are about avoiding what we don't want. Too hot, too cold, too hard, too soft, I don't like this; I'm resentful about that …

To know what is "just right," we have to connect with the truest part of ourselves. A favorite quote from *A Course in Miracles* offers clear direction:

"The journey to God is merely the reawakening of the knowledge of where you are always, and what you are forever."

How do we reawaken the knowledge of where we are always, and what we are forever? Two ways: experience and choice.

EXPERIENCING "JUST RIGHT"

The first is to give time to the kind of prayer and meditation that can produce experiences of where we are always and what we are forever. We can't figure this out with our minds. In fact, we can't get there from here. We have suspended everything we think we know and take a leap of faith into the mystery beyond who we think we are.

As I surrender in deep meditation allowing the layers of worry and fear to unravel, I experience profound peace. Gladly I slip out of the concerns of life and into the eternal embrace of my true being where I am always with God.

Mantled with divine grace, I experience my true essence of love. To my soul, love is all that matters. All I care about is loving God, loving myself as God loves me, and loving others. In the experience of this loving connection, I remember who I am and how my gifts can best serve.

CHOOSING "JUST RIGHT"

This brings us to the second way, the choices we make. Once we've had personal experiences of where we are always, and what we are forever, we have a reference point for what is "just right." Each experience of our true being provides a unique perspective of how to share our gifts of love through work, family and friends. With this perspective, we can make choices that strengthen our experience of this reawakened knowledge.

We might not know the bigger picture, but we can feel moment by moment whether we are moving closer to, or further away from love. Unconditional love. I call that God. When we are touched by eternal love, we are changed. More of our true being emerges.

THE GOLDILOCKS CODE

Here I am with the opportunity to change what I do for work. How do I discover what is "just right?" By asking questions like:

- What am I doing?
- Is it resulting in more loving connections with God, myself and others?
- Is it producing the results I want?
- What do I want to accomplish?
- What could I do differently?
- How can I more closely follow the call of my soul?

As we gain awareness through inquiry, we can eliminate what isn't working – the parts of life that are too this, and too that. I feel stuck spending too much time doing tasks that don't generate income and not enough time on the most important things. Why is that?

The Goldilocks Code invites us to delve into the unknown with curiosity and awe. It takes courage to explore this mysterious territory. Looking deeper, I discover hidden fears that stop me from announcing that I can help people experience Divine Love! An inner judgmental voice says, "how arrogant!" while a fearful part of me cowers in my story of what is wrong, avoiding the discomfort of talking to new people and exploring new opportunities.

But avoiding what we don't like is only a small piece of this puzzle. Of much greater value is recognizing the invitation of the soul. What is "Just Right?"

As I let go of my "too this's" and "not enough of that's" and gave up my hiding places, I heard my soul calling me to the ministry. I've been ordained since 1986, but never truly embraced it until now. Once my heart opened to this calling, I received a flood of loving energy along with the mandate from my soul to create a new "Angel Ministry" ordination program. Within a day, I received approval to start this program through The Gateway University where I was ordained.

While the big choices are important, the small ones are vital. What is happening within, moment by moment? Creating a new ministerial program is an enormous undertaking. When I feel afraid and doubt myself, how will I respond? Will I hang out in my excuses and stories about what's wrong?

Where do you get stuck?

STEP AWAY FROM THE BOWL AND CHOOSE LOVE!

Goldilocks to the rescue! We can take a deep breath and simply think, "Hmm, not true." Like tasting food that is too hot - Stop tasting! Put the spoon down and step away from the bowl to stop the spin of self-judgment, fear and excuses.

Then choose love. Go to the place within that is "Just Right." This place is always available. Forever. With practice, a few deep breaths bring us into this place of truth where we hear our soul's call. In the embrace of eternal love, our true being reveals what is "Just Right."

I am deeply grateful to discover who I am. My whole life has prepared me for this moment. I invite you to take this journey into divine love.

Rev. Kimberly Marooney, *Ph.D. is a gifted author, mystic, spiritual counselor, and radio host. She has helped hundreds of thousands of people worldwide open to God's love, heal and move forward on their life paths. Could you use some angelic intervention? Kimberly offers Angel Readings, Spiritual Counseling and Programs to help you experience the Divine. Her profound books are Angel Blessings Cards, Your Guardian Angel, and Angel Love Cards.*

Get your Free Angel Starter Kit at www.KimberlyMarooney.com or Kimberly@KimberlyMarooney.com or 831-419-3200

How Many Two by Fours Does it Take to Wake Up?

TERRI DIENER

Nearly 30 years after the fact, I had one of those ah-ha moments – I discovered that evolution began for me while I was still asleep. I was going along, blissfully unaware, working in a job that was mostly satisfying, being in relationships that were mostly fulfilling, dabbling in personal growth activities that were mostly worthwhile. Then curiosity struck.

My neighbor had been asking me to go to an astrologer with her for many months. I resisted, not being sure I wanted to get into something so woo-woo, even though I had been reading Tarot cards for several years. Then I began feeling a tug, a niggling little thought that astrology might be interesting …

The astrologer began telling me about myself. "You're deep. You have a unique set of values but don't talk much about it. You often re-invent yourself." At least four times I asked her, "How do you know that?" And she replied – "It's all here in your chart". Then she said something about the Aquarian Age, and I got even more intrigued. After all, I was a child of the 60s, when the Age of Aquarius was glorified in song. I asked her to tell me about the Aquarian Age in 50 words or less; I thought it got born and died while I was in college.

She sighed and said – "50 words or less? I teach a 15-week course about it."

By the end of that hour, I was a convert. Unknowingly, I had plunged into a world that was totally foreign to my traditional, conservative upbringing.

I was working for the state juvenile justice agency. A few years before, my public information job was cut out of the budget. It was a rare occurrence for an occupied state job to be eliminated, and I was freaking out. Security was my mainstay. That's why I was working for the state. Jobs were secure, health insurance was excellent, and retirement was good.

In the year between learning of my fate and having it actualize, a position opened in the agency's training unit. I never saw myself as a trainer – standing in front of groups, presenting information, working with people's attitudes. I was panicking. It was either transfer or be out of a job. I took the transfer.

At about the time of my first meeting with the astrologer, my supervisor informed the staff that he had budgeted money for us to attend trainings in new program material, and believing that the best employees are the happiest employees, he authorized any class we wanted to take as long as the agency could benefit from it.

I had recently become an acupuncture patient, and was fascinated by the 5-element theory of traditional acupuncture. My practitioner told me of a course that another of her patients was creating, using the concepts of traditional acupuncture with groups and organizations. I was intrigued. Certain that I could find some way to use it in my job, I signed up for the program.

Throughout that year-long course, I was learning and practicing how to let the energy of a group run through me, identify where in my body the energy was active, and then select interventions to move the group's energy in a specific pattern. The key was the energy running through me. Soon I was getting sick. The energy of the organization was extremely toxic, and I didn't know how to shake it off. By the end of the course, it became clear to me that I had two choices: staying in that job would mean either getting sick or shutting down; leaving would allow me to continue opening and expanding.

I felt like a living dilemma. Security had always been a priority, yet I was beginning to work in a way that was making staying in my secure job impossible. The energy of groups? The 5-element model? Energetic interventions? Who in a conventional world would buy that? The state agency let me work with it because I was getting excellent results in teambuilding programs. But what would corporate America, or nonprofits, or other government agencies do with the idea?

What would happen if I left that job and went out on my own? That thought popped into my head at some of the oddest times: in the shower, in the middle of a training program, taking a walk, working out in a karate studio … I would push it away, because, after all, security was the key.

Then, during one of the astrology classes, we were talking about transits (when the movement of particular planets and constellations in the sky would coincide with those in one's own astrological chart). The dilemma – leave or stay – was right in my face. I was about six months away from the classic mid-life crisis. The astrologer told me that if I were going to leave the job, to do it before the transit occurred, or the inertia that attended to it would keep me stuck at least until it was over (in a year and a half), and possibly for the rest of my working life.

Seemingly on impulse, I told my supervisor I wanted to transfer from my full time position to the one half-time position in the unit. He agreed.

I was ecstatic. I did it. I broke the security hold. I could do this until I retired, knowing that I had overcome a major block. I was out of the rut.

I was delivering excellent training programs and getting lots of recognition. But the niggling thoughts started up again: you've accomplished in 7 years what experiential trainers wait their whole careers to do; what do you want to do now – rest on your laurels or move on? I ignored that voice.

The agency was undergoing major change. People were being transferred, forced into early retirement, and fired for relatively innocuous offenses. I went merrily along in my half time position, untouched by the drama around me. I did occasionally wonder how I escaped it, but didn't give it too much attention. I felt secure, and that was what mattered.

Then our work changed. We were directed to monitor programs instead of present them. I quickly became bored and frustrated. Returning home after a particularly bad day, I felt myself getting sick – sore throat, watering eyes, etc. Then I heard a voice in my head saying, "Why are you getting sick? You know the mind-body connection. Are you tired? No. Do you need a rest? No. Then why?" And I said out loud – "I don't want to do this anymore." That night, recounting the day to some friends, one of them asked what I was going to do.

"I'm going to resign when I go in next week," I answered.

Within an hour, all of my symptoms disappeared. I gave notice and left the agency a month later. I watched myself do this as if it were someone else occupying my body.

I had no money in the bank, and two consulting clients. I comforted myself with the idea that I was fortunate – since I only had to take care of myself, I could afford to take some risks with my career. About six months later, the consulting dried up. I was supporting myself with a few coaching clients and reading Tarot cards in a restaurant twice a week.

I had no idea I was evolving. I felt like I was holding on by fingernails. I knew that what I was doing was right for me (just imagine what my family said when I told them I'd left the state job...) but I was really, really scared. At the time, the only thing that was clear to me was that the universe – or God – or whomever, moved me once (when the public information job was cut from the budget), and I would have to move me the second time. It was now a matter of conscious choice.

I opened my own management consulting practice, and enjoyed the variety and challenge for several years, but the constant scrabbling for business was getting weary. As I became idly curious about what might be next, my 15-year-old cat started having litter box issues. As a last resort, my holistic vet asked if I would consider talking to an animal communicator. Based on a photo of the cat and me on the phone, the communicator told me he was allergic to my shampoo, which created a chronic headache and a low level depression. She told me to put coffee grounds and fresh mint in a bowl and let it absorb the toxic energy. Within 3 hours, the pall of depression lifted from the cat and he returned to using his litter box. I called the communicator and told her – "I don't know what you do, but I want to do it, too."

Today, I am an animal communicator and executive director of an animal related non profit. Who would have ever thought …

With the benefit of 3 decades' hindsight, I realize that I answered the evolutionary call. I was dragged, kicking and screaming, into the best thing that ever happened to me. I am grateful for the cosmic two by fours that woke me up, and am decidedly delighted that I got out of bed.

Terri Diener has worked with people and their animal companions since 1995, addressing issues of behavior, grief, and animals in crisis. She brings to this practice a background in teaching psychology, counseling people and

coaching businesses in the areas of improving communication, creative problem solving, conflict resolution, and effective negotiations. Terri's first book, The Pets Speak, is now available.

Visit her website: www.petspeak.com

E-mail: terri@petspeak.com

Phone: 410-358-3954

Doing Well by Doing Good

GINNY VAUGHN

Have you ever wanted something with all your heart and soul – only to get it and realize you'd made a huge mistake? The first career choice I worked so hard to achieve turned out to be all wrong for me. Yet, my story shows how a different career transformed my life.

When my marriage dissolved, I was dumped into the job market with no skills or work experience. Logic told me I needed a college degree, so I could get a good-paying corporate job with security for me and my kids. Three years of full-time college plus a full-time job finally netted me that long-awaited diploma. At last, I got that "perfect" job!

It didn't take long to realize I was totally out of place. As a young female in a male-oriented industry in the early 70's, I was walking through a sexual mine field. Nearly every male I met made some type of "proposition." It was insulting, degrading and extremely frustrating. I also often performed above my job quotas, which created an uncomfortable jealousy among my male co-workers.

I found myself longing for my own business. I wanted to be boss, set policies and determine my salary and benefits. I was willing to work hard, and I wanted to keep the results of my hard work. I decided to make a list of what the now wiser me truly wanted and needed in a career. Here are a few items that were on my list so many years ago: unlimited income potential, travel to interesting places, flexibility in case my kids got sick, a company with a conscience, friendly co-workers, products that make a difference in people's lives.

I searched, praying for guidance as I went. I found many opportunities but none felt right for me. Finally, an article in Success magazine caught my eye and lit the fire of my imagination. It talked about a woman in a wheelchair who built a successful multi-level business with a reputable health and wellness company.

A multi-level business? Not something I'd even considered, but the benefits mentioned were those for which I'd been searching.

Now, the scary part! Should I trust the inner voice that was shouting, "You've found it! This is exactly right for you!" or, do I heed my fear and anxiety? Stay in the job that was making me miserable or risk changing careers and starting anew? What did I have to lose? A regular paycheck. Terrifying thought in my circumstances. What did I have to gain? An opportunity for great career satisfaction. Yes, but could I be successful? I chose in favor of the possibility of a happier life in an exciting, new direction. I know that choice took great courage, but, at the time, it was really the only one possible.

I had never heard of Evolutionary Women or a New Paradigm. I didn't know the world was on the brink of discovering a new way to live.

Nor had I ever heard of Shaklee Corporation. This new business, I soon discovered, turned out to be uniquely suited to my special needs. At that time, I was visiting an allergist twice a month for shots and medication. She had me on a very limited diet due to food sensitivities. I had no energy, constant headaches and felt terrible all the time.

In the early 50's, Dr. Forest C. Shaklee, a pioneer in the health and wellness field, created nutritional products from organic sources. These supplements contained bio-available nutrients. Feel better or get a full refund was the promise. I truly did not expect a couple tablets and a morning shake to change how I felt, but I was willing to test the guarantee and find out.

Wow! What a difference! Within a couple of days, my energy was boundless and I felt like a new person. I was quickly able to return to a normal diet, and I never visited the allergist again.

Another product line developed by Dr. Shaklee included non-toxic cleaners for home and laundry. Before the word "biodegradable" was in the dictionary, this extraordinary (Evolutionary!) man understood the hazards of grocery-store-type chemical cleaners and created nature-based alternatives. He knew we had a responsibility as inhabitants of this planet to honor Mother Earth and not abuse her. Because these products were not only safe for humans but also the environment, they became the choice of Jacques Cousteau for his ships, the National Earth Day Committee as their suggestion for every American household and Oprah who gifted them to her audience as some of her Favorite Things.

These unique products also played a special role in my life. For many years, I experienced severe migraines that began on Saturdays when I started my weekly house cleaning chores. My husband discussed this with our family doctor, who suggested I work with a psychiatrist to help me understand "why I didn't like to clean house." A year of visits to the shrink helped my self-esteem but the weekly migraines continued until I substituted Shaklee's home care products. Once I began using these non-toxic cleaners, the headaches disappeared and cleaning became a joy-filled experience. Apparently, for years I had been reacting to the chemicals in my household cleaners, and they were causing the painful migraines. Thanks to Dr. Shaklee, now I can save my health and save the environment at the same time. His pioneering insights were way ahead of his time.

There were other ways the products continued to bless my life. Embarrassing teenage acne that persisted into my 30's disappeared when I changed from department store skin care products to Shaklee's natural options. I began receiving compliments on my "beautiful skin" that utterly amazed me.

My thankfulness bubbled over, and I wanted to tell the world, which led to a new appreciation for why Dr. Shaklee had chosen network marketing as his business model. These products were different. He wanted to make sure they were introduced by a caring neighbor or friend who could explain how to use them and why they were so unique. As I shared my excitement about Shaklee's healthy product alternatives and this revolutionary business model, I was able to earn a full-time income working from home.

Those of us with an awakened conscience want to not only help our own families be healthier and happier, we really want to make a difference in the world. The way of Evolutionary Women is not just to share our excitement about a product, book, or new way of doing something; we feel most fulfilled when we can empower others and "teach them to fish" as well. Network marketing is the perfect business model for some of us because we receive financial benefits for doing what comes naturally. Dr. Shaklee chose not to pay for conventional advertising but, instead, to reward us handsomely for our word-of-mouth efforts. How ingenious and perfect for these unique products.

I feel blessed that my perfect career also gave me the opportunity to grow as an individual. I lived my life as an introvert – shy, reserved and afraid of most life experiences. I took a public speaking course in college. Shortly after the semester began, my teacher advised me to withdraw, feeling there was no way I could receive a passing grade in his class. Yet as I developed confidence as a new business owner, that fear of public speaking amazingly disappeared. When I'm speaking to a group, I forget about myself and focus on how I can help each and every person in my audience. It works like magic!

Owning my own business created special advantages. My home office saved me transportation time and gasoline dollars – two biggies today! I got rid of my alarm clock, my early morning commute and expensive childcare bills. I've even worked in my bathrobe. When a family member was terminally ill for several years, I was able to be available as needed. No corporate job would have allowed me to be by his side for months at a time and still pay me my regular salary.

When I think back to when I wrote that list describing my perfect career in the mid 70's, I had no idea I would actually be able to find a career that would be so very perfect for me. I've since discovered that taking time to make a list for whatever I want to attract helps align the powers of the universe to make my desires a reality. Only in my wildest dreams did I imagine that I'd find a business that would allow my family to benefit for years to come. Little did I know then that my daughter, Betsy, would join me! We've never been just mother and daughter, we've always been best friends. And now, we're even partners! We think alike and work beautifully together – the synergy truly makes our one plus one equal ten! Words cannot describe my deep joy and satisfaction.

I'm ever so thankful I read that article in Success magazine. And, I'm ever so certain it was no accident that I did.

Ginny Vaughn discovered a business opportunity like Shaklee Corporation created an enviable lifestyle. Sharing products and benefits with other women is a strong focus in her life.

Learn more at: www.shaklee.net/heartsanddreams. For free samples of her books Healthy Women, Healthy Kids and Ever Dream of a Better Life?, write to Ginny & Betsy at Hearts and Dreams, PO Box 423, Timonium MD 21094 or call them at 800-669-8162. They'd love to help make your dreams a reality, too!

Awakening to my Entrepreneurial Journey

CHRISTINE KLOSER

Growing up, I always felt like I was different. I didn't quite belong. Even though I excelled in competitive figure skating and was an accomplished dancer, I had an underlying feeling of not fitting into the mold of a typical New Englander. I rebelled against conformity and had an innate sense that there must be a different way of living than that which I saw in my suburban Connecticut town.

Perhaps that explains why I felt sick to my stomach when, as a senior in college, I dressed in a gray suit and black pumps to go on job interviews. Nothing about the suit, the pumps, the interview, or the "box" felt right. For me, the thought of a regular job and nine-to-five hours was an unappealing proposition. I had no idea what I wanted to do, but I knew a J-O-B was not it. I hadn't heard of entrepreneurship as a career option, so I was completely unaware of the world (and experiences) that were possible for me.

Thanks to college "senior-itis," I decided to enroll a few good friends in a plan to move to sunny Southern California after we graduated. Nobody believed we would actually do it. After all, nobody from a conservative private Catholic college would think of packing up the car and moving 3,000 miles away with no job, no connections, no place to live, and just enough money to survive for a month or two. However, for someone with an untapped entrepreneurial spirit and eagerness to experience all that life had to offer, this was the only logical choice for me to make.

After waving goodbye to my shocked family and squeezing into a Volkswagen Fox with two friends, a suitcase, a map from AAA, and a cooler full of snacks, I was off for the journey of a lifetime…a journey I didn't anticipate when we pulled out of the driveway. As we entered the freeway, I felt a thrill at the anticipation of the unknown experiences and opportunities that lay ahead for me. Even though I was still unaware of my entrepreneurial possibilities, I remember feeling that I loved taking this risk and doing my "own thing" rather than what society expected of a recent college grad.

The following year was all about fun! Heck, what college graduate wouldn't thrive in a hip San Diego beach town with nightclubs on every corner and beautiful weather all year? When I needed money, I got a one-month temporary job at San Diego's number-one rock radio station. This temporary job led to a nine-month assignment there. It was good to know I could have fun and be an asset to a company. Then, still unaware of the option of entrepreneurship, I returned to Connecticut to get a "real" job as an account executive for Hartford's number-one radio station. I think society finally got its message through to me that I should get serious about my life. For two whole years, I pretended I liked the job…until I was fired. I guess my pretending hadn't fooled anyone. Looking back, being fired was the best thing that could have happened to me.

Packing up the car again, I headed west—this time to Los Angeles. Finally, in Los Angeles, at the age of twenty-four, my life came together. By the grace of God, I fell into a job as a personal trainer, and within twelve months of getting started in the field, I launched my own private personal training business. Clients found me; so I didn't need to advertise. I worked only twenty-five hours a week, enjoyed my clients, made great money, and loved my life. I found my groove as a free-spirited entrepreneur helping people be healthy and fit. What more could I ask for? Life was good! Life appeared to get better when I had the opportunity to open my own private gym and yoga studio in an upscale location. After running that business for one year (working sixty hours per week and not having much fun), another opportunity surfaced: to take over a larger yoga studio. Naturally I said, "Yes!" And now my true entrepreneurial journey began.

Faced with $10,000 per month in overhead (not including my salary) and only $5,000 per month in revenue, I was in way over my head. Every other endeavor I'd embraced was easy, came naturally, and was fun...but not this one. I financed my payroll on personal credit cards; I figured out how to live on a poverty-level income; I was discouraged and isolated; I was on the verge of bankruptcy. I sat on my bed dialing the bankruptcy attorney on the phone, in tears, with my heart racing, and I felt like a complete failure, convinced I would never amount to anything in my life. It embarrassed and shamed me to make that phone call. It brought up a lot of fear, doubt, sadness, anger, frustration, and self-doubt. Maybe the entrepreneurial life wasn't right for me, after all. Maybe I just didn't have what it took to succeed.

Somewhere amidst the depth of my emotions, I knew this experience would either make me or break me. At the time I had this realization, I did not yet know about the multitudes of mega-successful entrepreneurs who also experienced temporary failure. It was before I understood the Divine Perfection of my journey, and it was before I embraced challenges as opportunities for success. Thankfully, a few years earlier, I started a women's networking group to connect with other like-minded entrepreneurs in Los Angeles. In this time of darkness and despair about my business and finances, I drew upon the energy of the women in this group. In their faces I could see I wasn't a failure and could access the gratitude I felt for every moment of my experience through this challenge. Through their mirror, something changed in me, and gave me the courage to not file for bankruptcy and make a conscious choice to have this experience make me rather than break me.

Two of the most profound blessings of being an entrepreneur are the power of choice and the freedom to create work you love. The journey I've experienced since making the choice to succeed has been a continual source of fuel for me to discover and be more of who I am, for me to experience freedom. During the seven-year journey of owning and operating my women's networking group (NEW Entrepreneurs, Inc.), I was stretched, challenged, and grew in ways I never imagined possible. I launched a successful seminar company, have helped nearly three hundred entrepreneurs become published authors through my publishing company, facilitated retreats, and hosted telesummits in which I interviewed experts like Michael Gerber, author of *The E-Myth*, Neale Donald Walsch, author of *Conversations with God*, Seth Godin, "America's Greatest Marketer" and Dr. Joe Vitale from *The Secret*.

The deeper I engrossed myself in the entrepreneurial journey (and discovered how to succeed as a "conscious" business owner), the more I embraced my true gift as an entrepreneur. My gift was to coach other entrepreneurs in embracing their journey, turning failures into successes, engaging their spirituality, and manifesting their goals and dreams. People often tell me that my experience with the yoga studio as an owner and instructor helped me develop the unique gift of blending intangible/Universal principles with tangible business strategies. Now I coach my clients in creating business strategies, gaining clarity on their vision, marketing plans, and product/service development...and provide them with guided meditations and grounding exercises to tap into the Universal energy that abundantly supports them in manifesting their goals and dreams.

When I set forth on my first cross-country journey, I had no idea where I would be today. It's difficult to imagine what my life would be like if I hadn't chosen to be an entrepreneur. Being an entrepreneur identifies me nearly as much as my role as wife and mother. Entrepreneurship is at the core of who I am and my desire to be fully expressed as my Self in the world. I am who I am today because of every challenge, obstacle, success, failure, dream and goal I've experienced along my exciting journey.

Christine Kloser is an inspirational business coach, engaging speaker, award-winning book publisher, and author of The Freedom Formula: How to Put Soul in Your Business and Money in Your Bank. *Since 1991 she has been an entrepreneur; continually exploring new ways to integrate her spiritual understandings with strategic business tactics for herself and her clients. She provides lectures, training, coaching, and book publishing services to thousands of entrepreneurs worldwide.*

You can get a free copy of Christine's Conscious Business Success Kit by visiting http://www.loveyourlife.com today.

The Razor's Edge

SARA WERBELOW

My mom (and guide in this lifetime) has often told me, "It is like walking the razor's edge." I cannot think of a better way to describe my experience in this life. I am thirty-six years old, soon to be thirty-seven, and I like to think I have the tendencies to be an aware and conscious being.

I come from a very mixed up crazy family of over-achievers, great academic and spiritual thinkers, world class networkers, money makers, and do-gooders: salt of the earth, all around good humans who have had their share of hard times and hard lessons. The varying degrees of consciousness (or lack thereof) within my small network of family and extended family are hard to fathom. You would think people who have been exposed to great study and world travels would be innately contemplative on a soul level. Often this has been widely apparent and other times it has been a great source of frustration and confusion for me.

Luckily, there has been enough contemplation and questioning in my family to offer me a door into my own awareness, which I opened at a young age. It has been open and closed since then. So now I am giving myself a voice on these pages for what I have witnessed and experienced. Thank you for going on this journey with me.

As I write this, I find myself poised at yet another threshold of understanding, more than understanding, because in some ways I have always understood. I know that there are parallel realities. I know that we are all on this path of understanding together. I know our Benevolent One is always present. This inviting awareness is best described as a meek opening to the exploration of honest thought and feeling.

I am at the sharpest edge of choosing to rest in this awareness right now. My life has brought me to a major turning point where I have a conscious decision to make. The circumstance doesn't really matter. Suffice it to say, it can substantially alter the course of my life.

The decision I am faced with is how much I want to feel what I truly feel. We all know every choice leads to more choices of varying magnitude. Yet, our awareness and conscious surrender to what is true can change what we witness and see and feel in an instant.

It is taking all of my strength to even open to the choice of a greater awareness of myself. Why can't I just look the other way? Why can't I just bury my feelings?

How can I be so tired?

* * *

I have brought myself to this place. I have only myself to thank.

It has been such a long life or perhaps series of lives. It is staggering to me to hold the infinite while at the same time feel the weight of the struggle. This is the razor's edge. It feels so very precarious on either side of the edge. Slip one direction and be held down by the apparent suffering, competition, greed, fear, and loneliness. Elevate the other direction and be floating high above it all, experiencing a simple sense of knowing that feels peaceful and certain. Feels right. Feels like coming home.

* * *

I would not change my experience of this blended reality, however painful it has been for me.

The nuance is strangely rich and comforting and familiar. I can feel God's warm smile and embrace. I know we are collectively safe and connected as one. However, it is a very lonely space, and I know in some ways we are meant to go it alone. Feel the pain, the hardship, the challenge. Without speaking, I ask you "Will you stay awake with me?" And when you stay awake with me, I do not need you to carry this burden for me. I ask you only to really look at me. Put your hand on mine and breathe through it with me.

On the surface I look just like everyone else. I have dirty blonde fluffy hair, a mess of freckles, a loud booming laugh and a firm hand shake...easy going...have it all together? I'm a mother, a wife, a daughter, a sister, a professional, a community activist, a friend and an average citizen. I am boring and simple. In a good way!

But right under the surface is my God-like expression, along with my desperate vulnerability, the ache of my heart. It brings me to my knees what I have seen and can see. The little child reaching up for her mother's hand, the first smile on a newborn's face, a friend's vulnerability, compassion of a stranger, the world's despair, humanity in question. The agony and the ecstasy of the human experience?

* * *

I am touched witnessing the vulnerability and sensibilities of my sisters and brothers in this lifetime. The razor's edge allows me to slip into two different versions of reality and consciousness at the same time. At times my double vision has weakened me. It has made me question and contemplate. It makes me feel stupid and unsure.

It takes my breath away and shocks my system. It renders me speechless, and I feel powerless. Powerless to have the courage to persevere, powerless to be a bold mother to my daughter so that she may see strength and conviction in my eyes. My daughter especially. She needs me to assure her that we can hold the "heart space." God and mother earth are depending on us to be brave.

I am a mirror for my husband and my son as well. They need the steadiness, the consistency. I long for the ability to carry the weight of this world all in a single breath, a single moment.

At times, I feel as though I am flying. Literally. All the muscles in my body are taut. I am neither feminine nor masculine. I can tap into these energies and part the seas. I know this is the true grace. This must be what the Bible speaks of in its stories of our collective strength and power. I'm meant to be a messenger and a carrier. It doesn't matter how hard I might try to fight the current.

I can see this clearly in my daughter's searching eyes. She is searching for something that carries us back to our tribe. I feel that my origins are a tribe, a band of sisters, sisters wandering, sisters in movement. I knew then, and I know now that we have to stay fluid and fearless, not depending on any sense of stability outside. Inside we are the stability allowing the changing nature of our actions and feelings and expressions. Letting it pass through us. Gaining momentum as we align with kindred energy.

I have often felt this quality of living heaven on earth. When I'm here, I'm in the utopia I have read about or heard about. I have the entire creation at my fingertips. It is a conscious choice for me because I am aware.

Sometimes I do not want to see it. I feel afraid. I want to slow it down. I want to be normal. I want to read the paper, see a movie, shop for my groceries, play trucks with my son, daydream about sunny skies and ice cream.

* * *

Dear reader, are you out there? Yes, I know you are on this adventure with me. And you will stay awake with me. I have to trust this sense of knowing that I am not alone. Whether we speak of this or not when we pass next time, I know you love me, and you can be certain that I love you.

I witness your grace and acknowledge your path toward awareness. You have helped me today to let the truth in. I will continue to wander the path and not be afraid to perch on the razor's edge. I have asked for this awareness and know that only sometimes will I choose the elevated thought. Yet, I will not shame myself in the times I get bogged down in my own suffering, for the two go hand-in-hand. Spoken in the words of Barbara Marx Hubbard, the razor's edge has been an "evolutionary driver" for me. Without one side, I cannot be awake to the other. Bless you.

Sara Werbelow resides in Park City, Utah with her husband Jeff and their two beautiful children, Madeleine (8) and Vincent (2). Sara is a Real Estate Broker with an MBA (which she got when she lived several years in Hawaii). She is now active in Historic Preservation and leadership in her growing and evolving community. Sara enjoys spending free time laughing with her family and appreciating the warm sunshine and fresh air in the mountains of Park City. Sara's mother and best friend, Bonnie Kelley (Co-founder of Evolutionary Women), has served as her incredible spiritual mentor and continues to introduce her to wonderful Principles of Life and Love.

PART FOUR

I Evolve My
Relationships

Learning to Let My Light Shine

MARY K. REDINGTON

I am an actor. While I learn all the time in my trade, I remember one valuable lesson learned one year while performing in my first professional acting job, 'summer stock', in the great state of Texas.

Summer stock is like paid summer camp for student actors. When your work, which feels more like play, because it is, in fact, a play, is done you get to hang out with people from schools all over the country. You sing songs from musicals all night long, lie out and get a tan, attend parties, and go on road trips. It's so much fun.

You must first audition, and then there are callbacks. You act and sing and dance for directors from companies all over the country. The audition process is a fabulous experience, and you learn so much just from being there.

Oh the joy when you get the call from the casting director! And I was picked to go to Texas. It felt like an elite club, and I couldn't believe that I had been invited to join. It's a big deal when you go to a small school in a small town in West Virginia and only a select few are chosen. I was on top of the world.

Texas was really going to be a blast! We would be there for four months. When I got there, as was my way, I made friends right away. Then, as was also my way, I stepped in it soon after. I was very young, still learning about the world and making a lot of mistakes. I would be loud and rude and I often told people what I thought without thinking about how they would feel (one thing I'm proud to say I have grown out of in my later years). I opened up too much too fast, and a few people got angry with me. People saw a side of me that they did not respect. Good friends whom I had made right away were barely speaking to me by the second month. I started to have a terrible time.

I called my mother, who gave me some very good advice. In this situation, she told me, I had three options: I could leave, just plain go home and live with my parents for the rest of the summer. I could walk around like a zombie for the rest of the time, not getting to know people and just finish out the season. Or I could continue on with the friends I still had and make the best out of my situation.

I chose the third. I would press on and enjoy myself. I would show these people who I really was inside and let them make up their minds at the end of the show.

That second half of the summer, I had the most amazing time. I hiked to the lighthouse, a rock configuration in the Palo Duro Canyon, and took a road trip through New Mexico. In New Mexico I saw the White Sands National Park and ran around in the sand, then I went to Carlsbad Caverns to see the bats take flight at sundown and finally toured the Roswell Museum. My sister came to visit, and we spray painted the Cadillacs on the Cadillac Ranch outside of Amarillo. My Mom and younger sister came and we went horseback riding and had a real cowboy breakfast. My Dad and Step-mom came out too, and we went to the West Texas Plains Museum. It was a whole lot of fun!

I also made friends with new people--that's the benefit of having a cast of 70 actors with a 30-person tech crew.

I became closer with a girl in the wardrobe department. It started because I was a mess with my hair, and one day she decided to come in and save me. She fixed my hair beautifully, and after a few days of me asking her to do it again, it became a regular event.

Every day she would come into the dressing room and laugh with us--the girls on my dressing room row--and fix my hair and listen to my silly stories about lizards I saw crossing the road or a crazy neighbor at the apartment complex where we were housed.

She was exactly the type of friend I needed in my life. She made me laugh, she yelled at me to calm down when I was getting stressed for no reason, as I often do, and she was real and open with me at a time when others weren't. Since we were housed in separate parts of the city and neither of us had a car in town this was the only time we had together.

We spent those two remaining months, talking, and hanging out at the show. It was great. I was myself with her and that was all I needed to be.

On the last day of the show, she came to me with a gift. It was a small antique tin full of tiny tins. Inside each tin were tiny little notes. "It is impossible to measure the value of the time spent together," was in a tin that said something about measurement. In a tin that was for gas and torch lighters, the note read, "You truly lit up my summer." And in a tin of universal valves, it read, "Your ability to 'spring' back amazes me." Then she included a long heart-felt letter about how valuable our friendship was to her.

Apparently, she had been having a hard time too. I had unknowingly provided her with a haven during the show. This wonderful person had saved my summer, and here she was telling me that I had saved hers.

What if I had given up? What if I had gone home and not faced my fears that summer? I would have given up not only on myself, and the wonderful growth that was there in Texas waiting for me, but also I would have hurt other people in the process. How dare I close myself off, how dare I keep my unique light from the rest of this world? You never know how much you'll mean to someone, you'll never know how much you can help, just by being yourself and being present in each moment. I had the opportunity to open myself up to the people who had closed off to me so quickly months before. Because I opened up to one person who really saw my true self, other people started to see me for who I really am as well.

That summer, I learned so much about myself, but what has stuck with me the most is this: to not give up when things get tough. Because you never know what you're going to miss out on, and likewise, you don't know who's going to miss out on you.

Mary K. Redington is an actor. In 2007, she co-founded the not-for-profit international theatre company Dramatic Adventure Theatre (www.dramaticadventure.com) She attended her first Evolutionary Women's Retreat in Maryland at the age of 23. Mary credits her mother, Andrea Hylen, for teaching her that in order to get what you want out of life you must ask for it, stand up for yourself, and treat others the way you want to be treated. She lives in NYC with her fiancé, Jesse Baxter.

The Magic of Women as Allies

MEGAN JOY HAVRDA

I had grown up in a very competitive, wealthy, keeping-up-with-the-Jones kind of town. I had been bred to win – the tennis championship, the art contest, the boy, the modeling job. In my town, women competed with one another on the PTA Board, at the country club, over monetary wealth, physical beauty and the latest fashions. Sure, women were friends, but I could always sense an undercurrent of competition that unsettled me.

Most women in that culture were catty, overly sensitive, and high maintenance creatures. I was warned not to become that way, and yet the behavior was all around me. I was raised to obtain and maintain the spotlight – we all were – and therefore, peer-ship was a bit awkward and often strained. I therefore spent more time cultivating my friendships with guys – they were simpler, funny, playful, and dependable. Years of this behavior resulted in two things: my mistrust of women and a stripping of the softer feminine qualities that I was born with.

Let's consider for a moment the power of places and their effects on our evolution. I have come to learn and sense that every place on the planet has its own geographic, historical, natural intelligence that brings its human residents certain lessons.

My journey of consciously experiencing women as allies would not officially begin until I moved to the Pacific Northwest in 1998. I now recognize that the Pacific Northwest is a landscape that inspires a return to community values and the responsible care for our natural resources. Its wild, lush beauty and palpable sense of community left me so awestruck and humbled that I began to open and soften after my many years of protective maneuvering.

After a few quiet months there, I met an entire group of evolutionary women, who at the time did not refer to themselves as such. They were talented, Renaissance-type women, a unique species for me. I admired and respected these women, and, they respected me to my core. No woman my age had ever done this nor had the capacity to see me for all that I was and wanted to be.

It was at this time that I recognized the power of gently reflecting one another for each other. This is a way of relating that means choosing to hold space for the truth, let the 'having to know and figure it out' impulse go, and have patience for accuracy to surface...no matter the circumstances or self-imposed timelines.

I watched these women experiment with this way of being, and though it felt natural to me, it still took me many years to fully integrate it. It was the unspoken foundation on which they performed all of their daily tasks: healing, cooking like professional chefs, growing gardens of food and flowers, fixing the plumbing, riding motorcycles, dreaming big, loving bigger, putting on a new roof, dancing 'til dawn, making a home, having children, generating abundance, and undoubtedly even sending their holiday cards on time year after year.

They intimidated and inspired me. They helped me understand that I could be sensitive, loving, creative and strong, smart, and independent, that it was not an either/or decision. They proved to me that I no longer had to mask or defend my femininity. They exemplified "community" and the woman's role in a healthy one, at that.

I blossomed in that fertile, luscious, real and raw community of Olympia, WA, and gained the strength and clarity to pursue my graduate degree and move to DC.

During that dynamic period I obtained five solid years of International Development experience and consulted all over the world for governments and NGOs. I witnessed many traditional communities--from the Sahara Desert's tented camps to Jamaican coastal towns to Bulgarian mountain villages--and observed how the women related to one another. They were firm, clear in their roles, gentle caregivers, tenders of nature, and the backbone of every society.

After several years of the laptop-in-hand, work-anywhere lifestyle, I could feel myself getting burned out and craving a gentler life. The flip side of my sexy international consultant's life was an ego-riddled, run me ragged, sacrifice me and my sense of life balance for planetary change drive that wore me so thin that I began to rebel.

The woman who blended her salads and drank them while standing up in the kitchen typing so as to keep focused and "save" time began making funny statements like, "Sure, I will go to that fancy event at the Inter-American Development Bank to honor the President of Brazil, but I will not wear panty hose, and I may or may not brush my hair." Some might call this self-sabotage, others might call it childish, but the truth was clear. I was done with the polished, politically charged, competitive DC lifestyle, and I was probing the ethers for my next right path, one where I could just be me – raw, frank, pretty, spontaneous, and wild – and grow the softer, more feminine aspects I had been admiring in other women along the way. Why couldn't I be that?

I could.

I began praying and asked for a calmer life and for one project that I could sink my teeth into for years on end (instead of a few projects in several countries all at the same time). My prayers were soon answered, and I organized a partnership between the DC organization that I had been consulting for and a famous archeologist that lived in Santa Barbara, CA.

I moved to Santa Barbara as swiftly as possible, of course, and the day I drove into town was the day that I met Barbara Marx Hubbard and Bonnie Kelley, one of the co-founders of EvolutionaryWomen.

In retrospect, this level of synchronicity is almost creepy! I had been moving through life trying to understand how to completely accept women as allies, and I walked straight into the Conscious Evolution Community and the birthing process of Evolutionary Women, the organization. I was even hired as a consultant! The saying 'we teach what we need to learn' certainly applied.

This was actually the beginning of the most painful and awkward period of my life at first. Being in the center of evolutionarywomen. org's manifestation was just the intense "in my face medicine" I required to experience the woman I had always been but never had a name for – an evolutionary woman.

Being labeled and referred to as an evolutionary woman has changed my life. The title itself continues to expand my personal capacity to take responsibility in this lifetime:

Now it is the year 2008, and I cannot sleep. I've taken the 'I will stay awake with you' mantra of the evolutionary women to heart tonight. I can feel us around the world – breathing, cleaning, caring, walking, working, laughing, eating… We are magnificent. And yet I am awake and disturbed because we are still holding back. I am still holding back. One question is keeping my eyes from closing tonight. It goes like this, "What if we all lived all that we are, every day?" This simple question could change the way humans live, regard one another, conduct business, and transform our relationship with nature to one of stewardship.

Consider what this might mean for you. I certainly am and know dozens of other woman who are sitting with similar renderings of the same question. We are women, and we shape humanity. This duty is becoming creative again, so let the spring return to our step; let us rejoice for the responsibility we carry together. We have each other, and we have our unique gifts to bring forth onto an empty canvas called today.

For **Megan Joy Havrda,** *business is play. Since 1995 she has worked in the fields of Ecotourism, Alternative Medicine, International Economic Development, Entrepreneurial Training, Real Estate Development, and Business Banking. Megan has visited and worked in 23 countries and is a relationship magnet. Megan is also a steward of a retreat center (www.hummingbirdlivingschool.org).*

Today, Megan consults for select projects that have the capacity to improve the human experience and care for nature.

STORY 33

Conscious Parenting

JEAN MOLINA

I am an evolutionary woman, yet I have made my career doing something that many people minimize. I am a stay at home mom.

That doesn't seem to be very evolutionary, I know, but it has been that way for me. My mother was also an evolutionary woman. She got divorced when most people didn't. And she worked, very hard. She had two minimum wage jobs that kept her busy almost every day and night. She worked holidays too.

I grew up strong and felt well loved by each of my parents, but I missed my mom. I had a big family. There were six of us kids, and I was second to the youngest. There were always plenty of people around to engage with, but still I missed my mom.

I told her that I wasn't going to leave my kids everyday like she did. I hurt her with statements like that. But I was young and angry and didn't understand what life was like for her. Do kids ever? All I understood was that I deeply missed my mom.

When I had kids, I decided, they would not have to miss their mom because I would be there.

And then I got divorced.

It wasn't a surprise. I had wanted a divorce since the first year of my marriage. My husband had implored me not to leave him, so I wound up trying to make it work for fourteen years. He was dear to me, and I thought that I could just stop feeling unfulfilled within the relationship.

In our third year of marriage, we had a baby and my heart doubled in size with the love that this baby awakened in me. My personal need for romantic fulfillment was forgotten. I decided that I could be satisfied being a stay at home mom.

Eventually, I had two more children, and my life felt wonderful. I wanted to give my children all that I had missed --along with all that I 'd enjoyed-- during my own childhood. So I cooked and I baked and I cleaned my house daily. I read to my children, and tirelessly attempted to answer all of their questions. I played with them and seemed to have endless patience. I taught them how to swim. I built a jungle gym and a swing set. I tucked them in at night and woke them with kisses in the morning. I took them camping and mothered their friends too. I was Super Mom, and I loved it!

Nevertheless, on some level I began to realize that I was on the path of losing myself, and that if I didn't do something differently I would end up lonely and maybe crazy, and in the same unhappy marriage. The kids would be grown and living their own lives, and I would become a statistic for the 'empty nest syndrome'. So, slowly I started to turn some of my focus towards my own personal needs.

When I was a young teenager, I had discovered a passion for Spirituality and New Age concepts. I had inherited certain psychic abilities that seemed to run in my mother's lineage, and I enjoyed helping people understand these kinds of things. I began to have many interested 'students' coming into my life. As part of my new commitment to my future-self, I started taking classes that would help me build on the talents that I seemed to have inherited. I learned how to connect with my own beloved spirit guides, and to sense others that had crossed over. I opened myself to the communications from Spirit, and was able to help people even more. I loved this work almost as much as I loved parenting my children. My husband, however, was becoming more and more uncomfortable. I began to talk about divorce again. I had no idea how I would make it work, divorcing my husband and providing for my children while still being available to raise them according to my standards, but eventually I had to take a blind leap of faith and just do it.

Unlike my mother, I was lucky. I had the education that enabled me to secure a decent job as a teacher immediately. I had two months before my job started and enough money to tide us over until then. So, in the mean time, I worked very consciously with my children to help them deal with the changes. Everything was going to be all right. And it was, for the first year, but during the second year, we began to suffer.

During that time, we were always in a hurry. During the second year of my divorce, I was bringing loads of work home and spending less and less time with my kids. I had also become involved in a romantic relationship with a wonderful man who seemed to be everything that I'd been wanting. The kids hardly complained, but I sensed their sadness, and knew that they were beginning to really miss their mom. Our hearts were aching and I could hardly stand it.

Eventually, my oldest son Nick started to act out and get in trouble. Finally, he was expelled from middle school. This, and the energy that it was taking to work, parent, and run a household alone was wiping me out. I was missing my children. I started to get headaches at work, and eventually I couldn't keep up with the load and lost my job. We were all so relieved that I was home again; there was no doubt about it that I was going to find a way to stay home, and parent.

It wasn't easy to make ends meet in the beginning, and I eventually had to sell my house. We barely got by while I struggled to find my way. I tried several paths that I had hoped would support us while allowing me to stay at home with my kids. I was determined, and even though it was difficult, we were much happier.

Then I began meeting more and more people who were interested in New Age concepts. They wanted help understanding Spirituality and Metaphysics. They wanted channeled information, and they wanted to talk to their deceased loved ones. I developed a workshop that I call Metaphysics 101 where I help to explain and explore basic New Age concepts. Eventually, as people got to know me, they became impressed by my passion for parenting (with the personal balance that I'd discovered) and to ask me for parenting advice. So I enrolled in a course and became a Parent Coach too.

Now I am writing articles about conscious parenting, and am working on my book: Metaphysics 101. I am available to my children almost always – and when I'm not, they have their loving father, in addition to the man that I had been dating – who turned out to be pretty great and now lives with us – adding his strengths to all of ours.

My mother's experience of parenting – although not ideal – succeeded well enough for her children. Some of the reasons for their success include the way that she and my dad treated each other. We understood that even though they couldn't make it as a couple, they did really love each other. Clearly, they loved their kids.

The way that they were willing to work with each other was evidence of that. For example, when my mom was at work, my dad was at our house. He made sure we had dinner, baths and bedtime routines. He was strict, but he was fair. I always felt safe when I was with my dad. He stayed with us every evening until my mom got home from work, and then he'd go on home to his place.

He made sure that we kept the family traditions too. During holidays he would come over early and start cooking. My mom almost always had to go to work later that day, yet both she and my dad made a point of being present at the table when it was time to sit down and eat. Aunties and Uncles were there too - bringing the cider and the sweets.

I adored my dad, and thought he was amazing. He was my first shining example of an evolutionary man, and I have always felt such gratitude for the gift that he was for me during that time.

As a child, of course I wanted more time with my mother, so I learned to find ways to get her attention. Acting out worked, but it hurt my mom so I tried hard to behave better. After getting expelled from Catholic school, my methods became sweeter. One of my favorite ways to get time with her was to offer to rub her back. She never said "no" to an offer like that. Then, once I had her attention, I would talk and talk and talk. And she would listen, and share her wisdom with me.

My mom was affectionate and caring and intelligent. She told me that I was funny and smart. She encouraged me to be strong and to know my own mind, and even during my divorce, encouraged me to follow my dreams, telling me "To thine own self be true". She was a very evolved woman, who encouraged my evolution as well.

My mom died three years ago. I held her hand as she passed. Her face relaxed into a sweet smile. I deeply miss her, and I realize how much I learned from her. I understand now, too, that her struggle to raise her kids helped me to discover my own passion: Conscious Parenting. My mom would be proud.

Jean Marie Molina is the Mother of three awesome kids, a Parent Coach and a Metaphysical Teacher. For the past 20 years, Jean Marie has been a Spirituality Consultant, a Psychic Empath, a Medium and a Semi-Trance

Channel. She has developed a workshop called Metaphysics 101, where 'New Age' concepts are explored, in a safe and fun environment. She is available for private and group consultations. Visit Jean Marie's website at www.onemoderndaypriestess.com

Mothers and Daughters

NANCY S. AYER

Myths are stories that enclose sacred and psychological truths. The stories, based on historically true legends or fictional narratives, are chronicled to explain a particular set of belief systems. Myths address our questions as well as offer us solutions to real life. If we look deep enough into ancient myths, we can discover ourselves in each of the characters and observe the relevancy of early patterns of behavior to our own problems of today.

The myth is one vehicle that allows us to realize we are not alone in facing our woundedness and the dark sides of our lives. In these stories, we realize that our journeys and our pains have been similarly experienced by even the earliest of human beings. Time does not alter human nature. Myths are meant to be fluid and exciting. It is only when they are taken literally that they become outdated and no longer relevant.

Conversely, when myths can be re-told, re-imagined, or re-visited, they become flowing, alive and juicy as they adapt to each new generation. If we are willing, a myth can bring a restorative and ever deepening significance to the various phases of our current lives.

The story of the ancient Greek myth, Demeter and Persephone, is a classic tale of the pain of separation between mother and daughter. In this legend, there are four main characters. I meet myself in each of them. The young hostage, Persephone, the mother, Demeter, and the wise woman, Hecate, represent the three phases of my life. I observe my own shadow side in the eyes of the fourth character, the abductor and ruler of the Underworld, Hades.

I discover I am the daughter who embarked on her own hero's journey and wandered away, seeking her self-empowerment and freedom from family, cultural expectations and adult conformities.

I am Demeter, the anguished mother grieving for the disappearance of her kidnapped daughter and agonizing over the loss of their former close relationship.

At this point in my life, I am also Hecate, the perceptive, astute older woman, who is unafraid to explore the darker side of things. Struggling through her own pain, Hecate has been strengthened and thus becomes the one who holds the light for Persephone's eventual ascension. The myth of Demeter and Persephone is my own story full of grief and anguish as I face the estrangement between my daughter and myself.

Carol Christ tells us that Mother and Daughter are One; but we are also Two. We are and are not the same. Through working with the Demeter Persephone myth I have come to understand that separation between Mother and Daughter is a form of death that is necessary for the growth of both souls. I find myself believing, however, that there must be a way for a daughter to become herself without rejecting her mother. I hold out hope – although bleak at times - that Mother Daughter love in all its strength and fragility may just be elastic enough and capable of stretching past misunderstandings, estrangements, jealousy, and guilt.

My following story is one of separation and is the first of what would later become two traumatic disassociations from my daughter. I write about these because I believe there is curative power in putting pen to paper, for both the storyteller and her listeners. When pain can be brought into the light in this way, problems may not be solved, but possibilities and spaces are created for understanding, personal growth, and healing.

The year was 1969. I was about to be initiated into the Demeter-like world of motherhood. Partially drugged, I was taken into the delivery room where I was heavily sedated. I was to have a second Caesarian section. Because I had my son by C-section two years earlier, my male doctor told me that due to his fear of the splitting of scar tissue, I was unable to have a normal birth.

The birth of my daughter was to be treated like a medical problem. It never occurred to me to question the doctor's thinking, thus my daughter and I became two more victims of patriarchal and archaic thought.

My lack of conscious living at that time prevented me from fighting back and insisting on a normal birth, as well as breast-feeding. I allowed the doctor to make the one and only final decision.

So as it was to be, in preparation for giving birth I was drugged, as was my daughter. On a prearranged date, my stomach was slit open, from hip bone to hip bone and my new little precious package was whipped out of me. I was not given her to hold, but told only that she was pink. I was kept sedated and had no contact with my newborn daughter for three days. Jaundiced, she was put under a harsh yellow light, cradled by the covers of a tilt-board and touched only by strange hands.

My breasts were painfully bound, their life giving sustenance dried up by a pill. I was the third generation of the victimized hushed and girdled era, that Victorian, don't talk, don't share, don't tell, don't know, don't ask, period of time where the doctors knew best, and where proper society ladies did not. My daughter and I both suffered helplessly from our premature detachment. Abandonment may, in fact, be the most significant trauma that humanity ever faces.

It is thirty-seven years later and today it rains. What could be more symbolic? Sometimes I feel the rain is God weeping as I do, weeping tears of sadness and tears of joy, poignant tears of remembering what was, hopeful and desperate tears of an unknown future. Rain weeps reminiscent tears of laughter and happiness and good times. It wipes the dusty film of dirt from all it touches and gives the tree frogs reason to sound deep, thankful croaks. It perks up the drooping moods of my crocus plants, and fills my cistern, but leaves my heart laden and my inner Demeter-like landscape barren.

Today's rain cries your angry tears and drops the message that you are moving from St. Croix. Dribbles of hope trickle down through the deluge as I recall an old Crucian expression: "In order to return, you must leave."

The ambivalent moving truck has pulled away carrying your possessions which tentatively await their new quarters in a distant land. I shall miss your very presence, but I know I must honor you and the new life that lies in front of you.

You are a beautiful, sensitive young wife and mother of two unique and extraordinary little ones. Take good care of them by taking good care of you. Do what you must, but always remember to hear your soul and honor yourself above all. In so doing, you will honor God and everyone else in your life.

Teach your precious ones, my dear grandchildren – the ones in your pain you only allow me to see reluctantly - to love the outdoors, to count the stars, and to feel the dirt between their toes. Teach them to watch the moon and see how it changes daily, as we women do. God is no less present in your beautiful backyard than in the warm pew of a church or in the depths of your own heart.

Go in peace my love, and remember I love you. Can you hear me? I know you cannot understand my pain now, but can you feel any of my deep love?

It is difficult for the Demeter in me to awaken and discover with Hecate eyes the powerful effect these two separations have had on me and now have on my daughter. My daughter is that inconsolable, angry, and abandoned daughter who suffers unknowingly. The victim becomes the victimizer and damages future generations unless some-one awakens to these truths. There is not much I can do now except to surrender to love, acceptance, and compassion and continue my own inner work towards a higher consciousness.

The bond of a mother's love and energy never goes away, even in separation or death. It is inherent in all humanity to return to our home, to return to the Great Mother. Losing my own joyous mother daughter relationship compels me to uncover new opportunities for meaning in my life. I pray I remain courageous. At the time of Persephone's abduction, the earth grew barren. Abundance returned upon her homecoming. Hope is enduring. Springtime, as it was in Demeter and Persephone's world, never fails to return. Hecate waits, knowing the myth is eternal.

Nancy Sumwalt Ayer grew up in Florida, graduating from the University of Florida in 1964 with a Bachelors degree in Education. She earned a Masters degree in Humanities in 2008 from Pacifica Graduate Institute in Santa Barbara, California, where she specialized in mythology, education and depth psychology. A Veriditas trained labyrinth facilitator having studied under the Rev. Dr. Lauren Artress, Grace Cathedral, San Francisco, Nancy facilitates labyrinths from coast to coast. Nancy is married to Anthony Ayer and they have three children and seven grandchildren. They divide their time between the Caribbean island of St. Croix in the U.S. Virgin Islands, where together they restored an 18th century sugar plantation, and Orcas Island, Washington State. She can be reached at stxnancy@gmail.com

Imagine My Surprise

SUSAN GARDENER

My maternal grandmother, Mimi, was a reweaver. For those who have not ever heard of reweaving, it is the repair of damaged woven fabric. It requires pulling threads from a hidden area on a garment and working them back into the fabric to re-construct the pattern. Mimi sat at a special weaving table, equipped with an overhead magnifying glass, and moved the short, harvested threads back and forth, back and forth, creating her magic. Reweaving is sometimes coined the invisible weave, and is fast becoming a lost art. As a young child, I was fascinated by the process and could sit by my grandmother's side as the clock ticked forward just watching her. Years later, I would find out that she had tried to teach several family members this skill that she possessed, only to discover that no one had the patience to learn.

The second of four daughters, Mimi was born at the turn of the century. Like many young women coming up during the first big war, she began learning her craft as an adolescent in order to assist her family financially. Cutting her education short, she went to work in a clothing factory by the time she was in her mid-teens. She married at age 23, late by the standards of the time period, to a man seven years her senior: an Irish Catholic sailor with a penchant for whiskey and women. Several years after she married, she gave birth to a baby girl, my mother, at age 26. Mimi's second pregnancy, at what would be considered an old age of 35, resulted in an undetected set of twin girls. In fact, one almost died, as the doctor had no idea until he was sewing up her episiotomy that there was another baby!

Shortly after my mother, Betty, was born, her parents, Mimi and Pop-Pop to me, purchased a tavern in East Baltimore. Being the only child for eight years, my mother was the apple of my Pop-Pop's eye. She was very social and took dance lessons, often entertaining the tavern's patrons with a dance or two on the bar, even at the tender age of four or five.

My grandmother was a hard worker. She didn't drink or smoke, but was around both for most of her life. She worked in the tavern kitchen during the day and did her reweaving in the evenings in their upstairs apartment. By the time the twins came, Mimi was full throttle into both jobs to help support her family of five. As a result, her children may not have gotten much of her growing up.

I, on the other hand, got all they didn't and more from her! I was the first grandchild, and the only one until my sister came along five years later. By the time I was born, my grandparents had moved to what would then have been called the suburbs. Since my father was serving overseas in Korea when I arrived, my mom and I lived with Mimi and Pop-Pop until I was almost three years old. My mother was very self-absorbed during my father's absence, and that meant that Mimi and I had a chance to bond in a way that my own mom and I never had.

Mimi was my biggest cheerleader! My mother was very young when she married, and without her military husband around, she was busy with her dance career and sewing some wild oats. With my unexpected arrival, my mother's exciting, fun life was abruptly arrested. Some of my mother's deviant behaviors would follow her well into my childhood. So Mimi saw to it that I got everything I needed and then some. The attentions that her own children missed out on while she had been so busy with life were passed on to me, and I felt her unconditional love surrounding me always. She made me a priority, and as I grew older, didn't judge me.

Now I would call my grandmother mild mannered. When she got mad, there were never any harsh words or yelling. She would simply say, "In about two minutes," and no one ever kept it up, whatever it was, to find out what would happen. There was just a knowing that you had crossed a boundary, and it was time to stop. My parents fought a good bit of the time while I was growing up, so being with Mimi in an atmosphere that was calm taught me volumes for later in life. Unlike my mother and grandfather, Mimi didn't draw attention to herself, and helped anyone less fortunate. It seemed that whoever needed a place to live for a while, Mimi jumped in, offering a space in her home. From people in her family, to people in her extended network, her house was a 'revolving door of hospitality.'

While I saw my own mother as selfish, Mimi was the giving care-taker, the sanity that I needed to feel loved. She always kept me on her radar as someone worthy of her time and attention. I feel that I owe some of my finest qualities to my grandmother. Without her guidance and influence, I know that I would be a much different person than I am today. She taught me perseverance in hard times, a solid work ethic, thoughtfulness and servitude. She loved her family and her faith. She felt like more of a mother to me than my own, and I was grateful to have her so close to me. I felt a safety with her that I often didn't feel in my immediate family circle. I considered Mimi to be a positive role model, and in many ways, my saving grace. She was my hero.

In my eyes, Mimi had always been my mom, the mom who may not have given me life, but gave me the life I came to have. I had the privilege of caring for her during her death process some twenty years ago, and upon her passing, felt that my mother had died. So imagine my surprise when I recently learned that my mother, Betty, was terminally ill. My mom has had emphysema for years from smoking, as well as diabetes, which runs in my family. She is now coming to the end of her life, and I am called to examine my own life in relation to her.

My mother is a character--some might say more of a caricature of a real person. Growing up, she was always louder than anyone else and could talk circles around most. Being right was important to her, so she could usually win any argument by being louder and talking longer than her opponent. She was fearless when it came to being in crowds. She would walk in confidently and command the attention of those in the room. Some of her qualities grated on me. There were times when I felt she was resentful that she gave up her dance career when she found out she was pregnant with me. I loved her because she was my mother, but I didn't like her very much. I didn't feel very safe or cherished. To me, she was the antithesis of my beloved Mimi.

I am now caring for my mother in this time of her nearing transition. I am watching the feisty, egotistical woman of my childhood fight for air to breathe from day to day. She is a shadow of her former self, as her body diminishes week to week. Hospitalizations are month to month, and there is no telling which one will be her final trip. It is never easy to witness the deterioration of anyone and especially a member of one's own tribe. It can bring each of us face to face with our own mortality and can bid us caution as we see what destructive living can manifest. My mother was no stranger to alcohol and tobacco, and now she must pay the grim price for hard living. I don't know if she will still be among us when this story goes to print.

The most wondrous part of this experience for me is that in my mother's decline, she is often nice to me. The compliments may not always flow out to me directly, but I know through others, and sometimes sense myself, that she is grateful for me. In that knowing, I am able to view her more clearly. I am able to transcend some of my past hurts and see exactly where some of her bleeds into some of me. Those parts of her are some of the best parts of me. While I may not command the kind of attention my mother garnered, I am usually confident when walking into a roomful of people I've never met. I may not speak as loudly, but I can stand in front of the room when I have something important to say. Though I've always thought of my sister, as more like my mother than I, I am the daughter who shares her love of words. I am beginning to have clarity about how much less rich my life would be without the influence of my mother. I am beginning to love her for more than just giving me life. I am finally seeing her in my own life, and welcoming the insights with open arms. The greatest gift is that I have heard the words, "I love you," more in the past several months than I can remember in much of my youth. And the best thing of all is that I believe it's true.

Susan Gardener is a spiritual peace minister, an evolutionary woman, artist, and mother to 3 teenaged girls. Much of her life's journey has been following her heart, leading and learning with her family and the organizations that have been meaningful to her growth. Most recently, she is caring for her terminally ill mother. Other endeavors include building peaceful community, and constructing a labyrinth on her property in dedication to the strong women who have paved her way. www.ThePeaceSisters.com Susan can be reached at spiralmama55@gmail.com

Editor's Note: Betty Anne Gardner spent the last few days of her life in Susan's home surrounded by family members. She passed away on May 30, 2008 with Susan and her sister, Donna, at her side stroking her hair and telling her how much they loved her. She was dignified and brave.

$\mathcal{S}$TORY 36

Watering the Seeds of the Evolving Self: Sharing the Healing Feminine Energy with the Wounded Masculine

NATASHA WESTRICH WOOD

"The Sacred Feminine is returning to the world through ordinary women who are carrying the healing power of the feminine and the Goddess back into the world.…" Take this "seed and bring it into a circle of women, nurture it with wisdom, give it energy.…let the tap root go down into the energy field of Mother Earth, to draw from and contribute thought and action to the morphic field, and then take it out into the world to bloom and bear fruit."
- JEAN SHINODA BOLEN,
URGENT MESSAGE FROM MOTHER:
GATHER THE WOMEN, SAVE THE WORLD

After reading Bolen's work several years ago, I began to look online for women's circles meeting in St. Louis. The idea of women gathering in circles struck a deep chord within me. After searching, I received an invitation to the Evolutionary Women's conference in Santa Barbara (August 2006). Planning to attend, I immediately called Bonnie Kelley. I could feel Bonnie's amazing energy of pure love pour through the phone, all the way across the country, spiraling out to reach me in the Midwest.

At the conference, I first began to understand the co-evolutionary process described by Barbara Marx Hubbard. Being in my early thirties, I was identified as a "younger" evolutionary woman, but I connected just as deeply to every woman I encountered, regardless of age. I experienced my authentic self, my highest self. I felt happy--in tune with the women around me and in tune with Mother Earth. And then I went home--my blossoms began to fade and wilt. I began to spiral downward.

I am married to a kind, empathetic, peace-loving Beta male who named our kitten, Gaia. My husband and I met when we were seventeen. My soul recognized him immediately. His experience was that I appeared to be glowing, and the rest of the people in the crowded room faded away. We both expressed that very first night that we would marry each other one day. After high school, we continued our relationship through college in separate cities. Just before college graduation, we became engaged. Once back at home, he was diagnosed with cancer. After having endured long distance and then cancer, we both believed the worst of our hardships were behind us.

Therefore, we both found ourselves increasingly disappointed that during our first nine years of marriage, things continued to spiral ever downward.

I felt my energy drain. When I looked in the mirror, instead of seeing a youthful woman in her early thirties excited about life, I saw a haggard woman worn down from the negativity destroying our relationship. As I wilted more, dark circles blackened under my eyes. I began to distance myself from family, friends, and activities. It became harder to keep our home in order, quite the symbol of the chaos in our relationship. Our deeply connected souls were becoming muddled with the muck of pain and regret.

This is the point where I eagerly ventured to California, excited about being with like-minded women. I could maintain positive energy there because I was surrounded and supported by incredibly high levels of nurturing feminine energy. However, when I returned home, the oppressive weight of the negative energy engulfing my marriage also returned. The destructive parts of my relationship with my husband were tarnishing the better parts of us. The pain and worthlessness of our wounded parts radiated out negative energy to our children, to those around us, and then seeped out into the world. I would wake up each morning wondering how I would make it through the day. I feared that the immense weight of the despair I carried would cause me to collapse to the ground. I experienced difficulty being fully present in the moment. Time slowed with sadness, each minute felt as if an hour. My heart ached. After a middle of the night trip to the ER for intense chest pain, I learned that 'broken heart syndrome,' also called stress cardiomyopathy, mimics a heart attack. It was confirmed, my heart was truly broken.

After immense work in effort to rise above the mistakes that hurt our marriage, starting with the evolutionary conference, continuing with my women's drumming circle to connect to the beat and life force of Mother Earth, breathwork, dreamwork, primordial sound meditation, and eventually conducting my own workshops to honor the Sacred Feminine through art (where I remind women that we each have a soul, a piece of the divine that deserves to be nourished), I was able to regain my Evolving Self, and this time not let Her go. I realized that in order to continue to bring what I experienced from the evolutionary conference into my daily life, I need to reach out to other evolutionary women on a regular basis; this is what fuels me and provides sustenance.

The strength of my own healing multiplied when in the presence of other conscious women, so much so that I was eventually able to share this healing Feminine energy with my husband, who embodied the wounded Masculine. Over time, he began to feel and respond to my desire to heal, which in turn cycled back to me and strengthened me further. Eventually, he too was ready to no longer wallow in the pool of disappointment of what did not go as planned. I had attempted many times to put the pain of poor choices that had hurt us both so deeply, behind me. He could finally see how he had been resisting healing and with this realization he affirmed that he was ready to join me, forgive each other, and live in the present. Subsequently, he made the conscious choice to walk through the doorway into the next chapter of life, where we can celebrate the joy of each day, the beauty of our children, and the love and tenderness (that continued to survive), which now thrives between us.

Today, my husband and I exist as a team. We envision ourselves as individuals, yet connected. We are two circles that partly overlap. I am one entity, he is another, but the combined energy of the two of us is yet another evolutionary force the world needs. Instead of bringing out the worst in each other, we are acutely aware that we have an ability to encourage, lift, and heal the other. To ensure this, each morning I invoke the highest version of myself, to bring about the sweetest, strongest, best, and most beautiful clear part of myself. We wake up with joy each day, simply happy to be with each other and excited about the upcoming day. Hours joyfully pass as if minutes. My heart is healing, and feels light, content, and happy. Our children, a barometer of this great evolutionary step we have taken together, also seem to be more joyful and more content, reflecting their parents' healing energy. Most specifically, we are motivated and excited about home improvement projects that we work on together, a positive symbol of the phoenix rising from the ashes of our pain and regret.

My message is this. To all evolutionary women, whether you attended a conference or not, if something or someone is weighing down your soul, fight all the more intently with this evolutionary driver in your life to stay connected and blossom into your evolving self. Balancing family, friends, work, and personal interests can become draining, especially if dealing with a strong negative force in life. When exhaustion or regret become overwhelming, being reminded that we are a part of something bigger than ourselves, helps us to persevere. That as much as we become tempted to close our eyes, we must keep our eyes open, and stay awake with each other. By being awake for each other, we become rejuvenated, our souls are ignited, and we will be able to advance the evolving process another ripple forward. Take comfort in knowing that this positive energy will reach and support other people who need strength. This very connection of positive energy with like-minded women and men collectively creates more positive energy, which spirals out to the community and beyond. By healing the wounded parts of our own lives, bathed in the support of the Evolutionary Spirit and by constantly striving to become our Evolving Self, we can contribute to the healing of the planet, one healed relationship at a time.

Each one of us has an important step to take us toward continuing our efforts as evolutionary women. We must continue to water the seeds of the feminine energy in our hearts, awakening in us a sisterhood of women, taking us to the fertile grounds with deep roots, which connect underground as they anchor to Mother Earth. To water our seeds is to feed our soul, which is to raise the nurturing, feminine energy in our home, our community, and our world.

Natasha Westrich Wood, MA, ATR-BC is an Art Therapist working with pediatric oncology patients at Cardinal Glennon Children's Hospital and St. John's Mercy Hospital. Natasha is an accomplished artist in the media of clay, woodcuts, papermaking, and photography. She plays with Jabula, a women's drumming circle, and performs for such events as Earth

Day. Natasha and Brendan live in St. Louis with their children, Ethan and Sarenna. Natasha@spaga.org

References:

Bolen, J. S. *Urgent Message from Mother: Gather the Women, Save the World.*

York Beach: Conari Press, 2005, pages 162 and 163.

Finding My Voice, and Finding My Community...

LAURA MACK

When I was young, I was an outgoing little girl. My mom recalls that I would chatter away to anyone who came by our home. I confidently entered elementary school, with my teachers commenting on my leadership skills. I felt good, self-assured, and whole.

But then life delivered a series of tragedies that gradually shut down my voice.

My father attempted suicide when I was seven years old, and although he survived, my parents separated for several years while he spun ever more deeply into alcoholism. My mother did her best to keep life as 'normal' as possible for my sister and me, but for me, a layer of shame settled into my core. Something about our family, something about me, felt wrong. My voice became quieter.

We all have our stories, some more tragic than others.

My dad's story is linked to my grandmother's story. My grandmother was one of the most influential women in my life. She both terrified me and thrilled me as a child, sweeping into our home with her enormous energy and authoritarian attitude—as well as a basket of homemade Latvian pirogs and apple cake.

Having been chased from her beloved country and forced to abandon her farmhouse and all her belongings as the Russians invaded during WW2, grandma lived her life with a fierce intensity—always prepared to defend what she had fought so hard to rebuild.

Despite living in a Displaced Persons camp in Germany for three years, and arriving in Canada with next to nothing, my grandmother's pride remained intact. Her firm resolve to rebuild her life created a beautiful legacy for our family: a garden oasis property in the middle of London, Ontario, and a lake cottage that gifted my sister and me, along with our cousins, with years of joyous childhood memories.

She started by borrowing a few thousand dollars to purchase a rundown old house on an overgrown, weed–infested acre property just a few blocks from downtown, along the Thames River. To pay off the loan, she rented rooms to immigrant Latvians, rebuilding her community—and also her wealth.

When grandma was 98 years old, and Latvia had regained its independence, grandma flew on her own back to her home country to reclaim her farm property that had been confiscated by the Russians. This was a trip that was against my aunt's wishes (my father had long since passed away from a heart attack, or perhaps it was a broken heart since he didn't live to see Latvia again), but grandma went anyway. Always a woman with a voice, she even gave a talk on life as an expatriate in Canada while she was in Europe. Turning her property over to relatives still living in Latvia was one of her final conscious acts before she slid into senility, finally passing away at age 104.

Throughout her life, her voice rang out, clear and true, despite the horrors she'd faced, the disappointments, the losses and the challenges. She was an inspiration to me—more so as the years pass. I now have a deeper understanding of the challenges she endured, and how she fought to rebuild a life for her family.

Although her strong, willful side was perhaps most obvious, I also know she fought depression at times. During our hours together in the garden, picking raspberries or pulling weeds, she shared how at times she wept with the overwhelming reality of how much they'd lost, how hard it was to build a new life in a new country.

But, where my dad drowned his sorrows in vodka, my grandmother dug deep within herself, overcame her fear, anger, and disappointment, and found a way to rebuild.

At my grandmother's funeral, my uncle asked me if I'd like to say a few words during the ceremony. I was struck with my familiar terror at the thought of speaking publicly.

"No." I shook my head. "I can't."

As our family filed into the pews, I looked at my grandmother's casket, and then out at the gathered mourners. How could I NOT speak about this amazing woman and her influence on my life? I leaned forward, hearing my own voice as a whisper in my uncle's ear. "I've changed my mind."

On that particular day, I connected deeply with the spirit of my grandmother, the community of Latvians and, of course, with my family. I found my voice when I connected deeply with my heart and my passionate love for my grandmother.

My voice rang out, clear and true. I shared memories of our tender moments, of our talks in her inspiring garden, of the disagreements we had, of the guidance she gave me. I felt the laughter bubble up, and the tears flow. My grandmother was alive in my soul, where she'll reside for the rest of my life.

And this has been my truth: I found that the way back from the pain of my own inner isolation has been to connect with community; a community that will hold the sacred space for my voice to come out, even if it's initially as a whisper.

I've been blessed to find many of those communities over the years, communities that have nurtured my healing and called forward my voice.

I attended my first Evolutionary Women's Retreat in Maryland in the spring of 2007. During that weekend, thousands of miles from home, it became apparent that weaving together an international network of empowered women was part of a larger plan that was emerging in circles of women; not just in Vancouver, British Columbia, but also in Baltimore, Maryland.

Women's networks, such as Evolutionary Women and Women of Vision and Passion that I co-founded in Canada, provide us a safe community to connect with the Divine Feminine and to explore ways of connecting with other women that may not exist in our families, our workplaces or elsewhere in our communities.

And it is in these communities of women who are gathering to support one another that many of us are, for the first time, finding our voice.

When I was at the Evolutionary Women's gathering on the eastern side of the United States, I rarely found myself thinking that I was with women from another country. Our commonality, not our differences, defined us. Borders fell away as I listened to women passionately share their visions for bringing about change in their world. I was with sisters who cared as deeply as I do, as the women in my circle in Vancouver do, about better education for our children, better access to health care for all, better government, helping our disempowered sisters, elsewhere on the planet we ALL share. All these women's voices. So beautiful. So powerful.

I'm honoured to be one of the first Canadian woman's voices to be heard within the Evolutionary Women's network. I often feel as though my grandmother's voice is speaking through me. I do know that her story has in many ways become part of my story, connecting me deeply to the women in our world who have struggled, who have been oppressed, who have had to flee their homes. Her ability to fight for, and to create a new life, has empowered me with an ability to find my voice, and to use it to serve.

Since I was a teenager, the word Namaste has resonated deeply with me. There are many interpretations of this beautiful Sanskrit word, but my favorite is: "I honor that place in you where the whole Universe resides. And when I am in that place in me and you are in that place in you, there is only one of us." This interpretation brings Spirit into our acknowledgement of one another, and infuses my way of Being in the world.

Namaste.

May we all honour those who came before us. May we all find our voice. May we all be empowered. May we all connect to a loving community. May we all find

Peace.

Laura Mack *is a facilitator who enjoys co-creating inspirational and transformative communities. Currently, she is working in Partnership Development with the International Leadership Association. She has been the executive director of a Canadian national association and operated a sole proprietorship promoting inspirational speakers, leadership and development facilitators and trainers. Mother of a gifted child, she is currently the Secretary of the Board of the Gifted Children's Association of British Columbia. Laura's passion lies in assisting individuals and communities achieve their potential. Whitelight Consulting lauramack@telus.net*

Sex Goddess of the Universe

JUDITH WATSON

I was actually fifty-two before I got some inkling of what it must mean to be a young male. Wherever I was at that point in the pre-menopause process, my hormone levels were undoubtedly shifting, and I suspect that I suddenly had more testosterone than I knew what to do with. I have never been so horny in my life. I would lie in the bathtub at night and find myself wondering what it would be like to give my body totally to someone. Sex was virtually all I could think about. I wanted to try it in new ways. I wanted to be Sex Goddess of the Universe, a title that had never so much as crossed my mind before. I lost any sense of moral objectivity and was kept chaste only by circumstance. It was incredible. Not exactly incredibly good, certainly not incredibly bad, just incredible.

I was working in a bookstore at the time and eventually started taking furtive looks at the sex books. They really weren't very good. Some were deliberately trashy, more designed to arouse than instruct. Some were translations--extremely difficult to follow, even with illustrations. The more I read, the less I really knew, except for one thing--desirability is actually created as much by your attitude as anything. If you make love with genuine delight, you will out-perform any expert.

Because I'd started having serious intestinal difficulties, which no doctor could find a cause for, I happened to see a psychic healer. "Oh, Honey," she said to me sympathetically, "You haven't even scratched the surface of the sexual energy you need to release."

Try sleeping with that diagnosis when you're fifty-two, and any further sex in your life appears to be out of the question.

In this case, however, I'm happy to say that when the pupil was ready, the teacher appeared.

We'd met a year before, business associates exchanging e-mail addresses because we'd enjoyed talking to each other. Then something prompted him to get back in touch, to call one night, out of the blue, to see how I was, and I suppose some part of me started then and there to tell him. He wasn't even in the neighborhood; he was almost a thousand miles away.

As it happened, we would write to each other for almost an entire year before we saw each other again. Because we both love words, and we both longed for someone with whom to have meaningful conversation, our friendship grew in cyberspace, always thoughtfully composed, answered patiently, written when we were at our best and most interesting, often twice a day, sometimes even more. There was nothing we couldn't discuss at such a safe distance. That correspondence was a joy and a diversion, both in the reading and the writing. It was months and months before we came to understand it was also a prelude and a foundation.

By that time, my hormones were back in better balance, but I also had a new appreciation of the opportunity at hand. If you're going to have an affair, you might as well go for the gold, especially when you've come to believe your last chance has passed you by.

For the vast, vast majority of us, no one in our culture, not our parents, our teachers, our therapists, our spouses, no one tells us that we are sexual beings. Our sex ed. classes have become more and more graphically explicit in our schools; our magazines more and more suggestive. We are warned about this, that, and every other thing, from the sanctity of our reputations to sexually transmitted diseases that have become life-threatening. Pornography, with the advent of the Internet, is everywhere.

But tell me, please, if anyone, anywhere, at any time, has spoken to you of sexual joy and wonder?

Don't misunderstand me. I am not advocating promiscuity, or random, irresponsible coupling for its own sake. I am talking about waking up, admitting to, and sharing one of life's most extraordinary gifts.

There are many ways for humans to relate to each other, and many, many forms of love. There are also an inordinate number of hang-ups, confusions, misconceptions, and perversions about sexual relationships, primarily, I would suggest, because of the conspiracy of silence around the subject, even now that we talk about it all the time!

Let me give you an example.

At one point, this lovely man wrote and told me that it turned him on to look at catalogues of women's lingerie. I cannot tell you the alarm bells that went off. "Ha!" said a voice. "That clinches it. He's obviously a pervert. Boy, have you been taken in." Perverted in what way exactly, I couldn't have told you, but the bells were insistent.

Well, okay. I had some choices. I could listen to the voice and back out of the correspondence. I could confront him, and say or ask what, exactly, I wasn't sure. Or I could weigh everything I knew about all the hundreds of things we'd talked about, all the things he'd said I agreed with, and simply trust that this confidence was offered in the same spirit as the others, with candor and without land mines.

I talked to myself about it for two full days. Then I accepted it as part of who he was. Period. I knew I had to either mean it or be done. And, I knew I had to mean it permanently, wherever it led.

Never had anyone ever talked to me about accepting another person's sexual idiosyncrasies. There was "normal," and there was "weird," and, quite frankly, I had no clue where one began and the other left off. Better to stay within the "normal" and not have to risk anything else. My own husband had discouraged me from anything very exploratory, so my experience told me that risk-taking wasn't welcome. And yet, this virtual stranger had become important enough for me to consider otherwise.

As the time grew closer, I had many anxieties about this affair-to-be, how I would perform, and whether--and in how many ways--my body would betray me. We're given no help there, either. So much cultural attention is given to fixing or masking the way we look or feel or smell, we have no idea how to accept ourselves and each other as we really are, and we go to a place of shame for things we can't change, which then fuels the problems, confusions, and the fears of genuine intimacy.

He was wonderful, simply, unbelievably wonderful. I do not know where he learned such total acceptance of the human body as it really is, but it was a gift to me beyond the imagining. He made love to me for two weeks straight. He took me again and again, just like that, urgently and repeatedly, at all hours of the day and night, as though being inside me finally righted some great cosmic imbalance.

He'd walk me, topless, out onto the terrace and stand behind me, enfolding me in his arms, firmly cupping and kneading my breasts as though they were made of some kind of sacred erotic substance from the gods to be used for healing and blessing for us and the entire world. Perhaps they are.

At his request, I'd wear lingerie into the shower with him. He'd watch as it got wet enough to cling to my every curve, then reach out with one strong hand, and in a single motion, rip it off me into nothing but a wet rag to be thrown away. Then he'd wash my body, sometimes with the soap on his own. I'm here to tell you I have a whole new appreciation for lingerie catalogues.

One time he lit the bedroom in candles and got out massage oils. He spent hours loving me with his hands and his voice, relaxing and exploring me all over. Other times were playful, and one night we got fits of the giggles under the covers like two nine-year-olds.

Being valued as a lover isn't just about sexual activity. He would brush and dry my hair. He escorted me to dinner both in five star restaurants and neighborhood cafes. We also talked for hours on end, wonderful, rich conversations about all manner of things, including matters spiritual, healing and transformational. There most assuredly is such a thing as an Evolutionary Man.

You'll wonder, I'm sure, where on earth I found such a lover/teacher as I did and where the supply house is. The truth of it is a paradox: he was there all along, but he didn't exist until I invited him, just as I was never in 10,000 years a candidate for Sex Goddess of the Universe when we first met, but she must have been part of me all along and finally got fed up with being denied and hidden.

We're all unique, and we'll never know in what ways that's true sexually without taking some voyages of discovery. From my experience as the Lady of Testosterone, I have some genuine appreciation for the traditionally male perspective that sex can be wonderful in its own right. But for me, truly great sex comes from complete mutual surrender, which can't happen until you learn to hold each other in a place both safe and sacred. What I needed more than anything else was permission to discover my total self, all of Judith, including my sexual self, admit she was there, liberate her, and ultimately, to celebrate and cherish her. So here I am.

And by the authority I claim from my own experience, I hereby grant you permission when and as you wish to do the same for yourselves. The more sex divinities we can foster, both male and female, the happier, healthier place the world will be.

Judith Watson. *The past several years have been the most extraordinary of this life so far. Their relationship has taken Judith and her partner on a wondrous spiritual journey including several continents geographically and more than one teacher brought to them along the way. Most fascinating of all has been the journey inward and the bond they have formed and refined as they helped each other to leave a familiar paradigm, grow beyond it, and become new.*

PART FIVE

I See a World That Works for Everyone

Water

LIZZIE RED

Water seems lately to define my life. Fluid, ever changing, varied, expansive and powerful. The very matter that holds all my fears simultaneously has the ability to wash them away.

What I now realize is that my fear of water represents a fear of my own hidden power and the uncertainty of life itself. There are no rules or structures to define me under water or decide my path.

Yet that reality threatens my very existence. The magnitude of what it holds beneath - unseen and unknown - overwhelms and consumes me.

To love water is to love the fluidity of life.

I've been swimming against a current for two and a half years now. Stuck solitarily out in the middle of an ocean, alone and waiting for the next wave to pummel me. I've been drowned in tears so long, I seem to have cried myself an ocean and created my very own waves.

I wanted to trust that the motion of these waves would move me somewhere I was destined to be and that place would feel just right. I have believed in everyone for answers-everything and everyone but myself. No wonder I felt lost, I was…

Realistically, I have probably been treading water in a cesspool my entire life, peering around so much, I could never really rest inside myself. I have always been this girl. This shell trembling, spitting water, swimming laps in a closed pool, to keep myself from recognizing that I wasn't moving anywhere that I really cared to go.

Then one morning, it's as if the motion stops, and you are so empty. Lifeless. Sobbing. Stuck.

It's when the world could care less about comforting you that you realize, the only way that you are going to make it, is if YOU make it.

Knowing this was a scary thing, though I would come to discover that not knowing is even scarier.

* * *

This all started, my truth emerging, at the very brink of my stepfather's death. He was always the catalyst of my despair - the tester of my strength - and yet my biggest supporter preceding his death.

I remember the last day I saw him truly alive. He had been sick for one long year.

I was fighting against my yearnings not to go to work when my car died. Since it wouldn't start, I called "out", to my work's dismay, and went to the hospital for the first time. I sat in the coldly lighted room with my stepfather while my mom spoke with the doctor. We silently watched television, just as we had for years before.

We hadn't spoken in months. We had always been distant, but his sickness had just exasperated our relationship. I was terrified, as terrified as he was, and I had disappeared during his battle with cancer.

Silence permeated the room that day, until all at once, he looked at me blankly and said, "I'm dying," as if in total defeat. And me, so frozen and broken, had nothing but brilliance to offer. "I know," I said, my face streaming with tears.

That was the last day that he was conscious. And I will never forget the fear and destitution in his eyes. He wasn't ready to leave earth, not nearly.

I feel that at some point life becomes a collection of flashing moments, and that is all that really matters in the end. Split second memories, full of life, that you will remember everything about… right down to the touch and smell of … forever.

I maintained composure after his death for a few weeks; then I quit life for a while. There were months full of couch vegging, daily kvetching, and reality show studying before I felt even slightly moved to enact a plan. I was sick of living for everything and yet nothing that had any real meaning to me. I became obsessed with the end of the world, which I convinced myself would occur in 2012.

I began to look at my life as though in a mirror. I saw everything that I was and mostly what I wasn't. I beat myself up. I bruised my own heart. I created battles in my mind. Mostly, it became clear that this was all I had ever done. And more so, all I knew how to do.

But I also saw a new and unclear path. What would I do if there were only six years left of my own earthly existence? Where would I want to be, and how would I leave my unique mark on the world? Life without my soul purpose, something I craved from dawn to dusk, was no way to live. Living for myself, I concluded, valuing my own sacred gifts, seemed the only way to participate joyfully in life.

* * *

I have this vision of being a new kind of success, generating income for the good of humanity. Connecting all species and valuing their inherent rights, so that they can find well-deserved peace of mind like I did. Creating a world that generates hope instead of damage in our lives and earthly surroundings… recycling at baseball games, organic corn dogs at the State Fair, yoga classes in our city schools. Solving problems before they exist as such.

I've come to this epiphany, silly as it may seem, through the eyes of the dogs at my feet, the flowers on my porch, and likewise everything living and breathing throughout my surroundings. I watch and witness daily; these beings mimic my intoxicating values, for better or for worse. The water, the energy, the force wading inside me, is stirring, and I see it through their eyes. They remind me still that I am capable, and that truthfully, I am not alone. I just choose to be.

The nameless, still and wise members of this earth, are my guides. On a daily basis they wholeheartedly reveal the devastations as fully as the joys of life. Their needs and centers are ever changing and evolving, and so I see through their reality, that life isn't planned. It is rather discovered every morning when you wake and adapt to the day's routine.

I now know that what grounds me is my connection with all living beings, shapeless and wordless alike, not academic degrees and ten-hour workdays.

And my purpose is greater than lists, anger, and expectations.

Through awareness, and the courage to see myself as I am, I've found that I hold the power to evoke change, simply by making choices and committing to the ripples I form. And as I create change in myself, I create change in my world.

* * *

Speechless hums
As the fan spins shadows
Around the dark

I was a lion in the dream
Braving fears
Catching wrongs
And chasing rights
Stiff hearts beware
I am open

Alive
Screeching
For midnights owl
Who prowls the openness
Of tomorrow

* * *

I have always known what I stood for and have stood tall, believing for many years in structures, frames and rules that no longer suffice. It is interesting that when I let my grip loosen on "what is right for me", my soul path unfolded before me. My acceptance of the fluidity of my own life, allowed me to write about this journey. The tides do change and I have accepted this.

My existence in this story doesn't have an ending, any more than it has a true beginning. I created a storm inside myself because I was ready to be cleansed.

I was never alone and not lost, for I was just focusing on where I wasn't, instead of where I was.

Interesting enough, our bodies are made up of 70% water...so it seems the power has been within me all along. The space I hold is formless and has no definition. I seldom contain regrets or expectations. I am changing daily and that... is just fine with me.

Lizzie is currently living in Prescott, accomplishing dreams bigger than definition. Along with her Shaklee business, she is most passionate about the Organic Food Revolution, taking her dogs to the park, her new adventure at Prescott College and mastering Dahn Yoga. More so, she is

awakening and becoming aware of her own power. Other than being on a mission for a revolution of society, slowly but surely-she is rediscovering her two long lost loves: dancing and writing. She strives to live life daily with a reminder of the quote, " We don't see things as they are; we see them as we are". She can be contacted via email at: be.saanti@gmail.com for website or other information.

Waking Up

GINA CAWLEY

A number of years ago, I was sitting at a traffic light in Orlando, Florida. Three of the four corners had gas stations, and until that day the fourth was a beautiful corner with palm trees, bushes and birds. But that day there were huge yellow machines ramming the trees down with great noise and violence, and in the background a "coming soon" sign for another gas station. I burst into tears. I felt the pain of the trees - I literally FELT a deep ache inside me for the destruction I was witnessing. I felt overwhelmed with the insanity of destroying this little corner of beauty so that another gas station could be built. I pulled into the parking lot at work and sat for a while until I regained my composure. I couldn't go inside and admit that I was crying because they were taking down trees and building a gas station. That's just crazy…. But now I know that I was not crazy – I was beginning to awaken to a new level of consciousness and a new understanding of who I am in relationship to Earth.

In my childhood, my family and church were my guides. As a young adult, I became aware of social justice issues and how my decisions had an impact on other people in my neighborhood and around the world. Then I was introduced to local and global environmental issues. I struggled with what to do with my life and how to be of service to the world. All of the problems seemed so important, and I couldn't decide which was the most important for me to focus on. I saw them as separate problems with separate causes and separate solutions… Now I understand that this struggle was also about a larger worldview that was struggling to break through in my consciousness.

In the late 1990's, I was introduced to the writings of Thomas Berry and Brian Swimme in their book, *The Universe Story*. Suddenly, all the pieces started fitting together. The Universe is one ongoing process, Earth is part of this process, and human cultures and human struggles emerge as part of this process. There is a fundamental unity, a deep Oneness that is the foundation of all that is. There are no separate problems or separate solutions – everything is connected. Once my context expanded to include this awareness of the Oneness of the whole Earth and Universe, I saw my life choices in a much different way.

I remember being taught that much is expected of those to whom much is given. As a young person, I understood this to be about how I used my money, time and skills. I had the opportunity to receive a good education and get a good job – so it was my obligation to use these to make the world a better place. With my new eyes, I began to perceive a deeper meaning for that teaching -- an obligation for the entire human species to awaken and take our true place in the journey of Earth. And I came to see my life as part of that process.

The human species has been given so much – we are the species that is aware that we are aware, that can reflect on our feelings, that has incredible intelligence and creativity at our fingertips. But during the last two hundred years, some of our gifts have been used in a way that has taken us down a path of destruction. I feel deeply sensitive to the suffering of the planet. Just as I felt the pain of the trees coming down for the new gas station, I am deeply affected by the destruction that our species, and particularly our culture, is bringing to the planet right now: the pain and suffering endured by animals raised in factory farms so that we can have $1.00 hamburgers; beautiful, diverse ecosystems and indigenous communities being destroyed by corporations planting coffee monocultures to support our Starbucks habit; our excessive consumption and all the species that are going extinct because we have destroyed their habitats to make more stuff; the great human suffering in Darfur, Iraq and countless other places around the world; the list is endless.

Some days it feels like more than I can bear, and it's hard not to feel anything but despair for the world. I find myself in angry and judgmental conversations. I am frustrated and impatient with the fact that humans continue making choices that lead to suffering and destruction when we should know better. I am terrified about whether or not we will make enough changes to avoid the worst predictions of global calamity. When I get stuck in my smaller worldview, I feel desperate, hopeless and cynical.

When I find myself in these moments, I know that I need to move to a place of understanding that the only person I can change is myself, and that just as my awakening continuously leads me to make different choices, the same will happen for others. I declare my intention to stop judging myself and others for not doing enough fast enough – to accept what is, to do the best I can each day to make conscious choices, and to not be attached to the outcome.

The fact is that I don't really believe that we are destroying the planet because we are inherently bad or greedy. I believe that it is happening because our understanding of what it means to be human has not developed as fast as our power. We have been shaped by the belief that humans are separate from the rest of the species and Earth, that we are the dominant species, that the resources of the planet are just here for us to use, and that technology will save us from whatever problems come up.

The good news is that science is now teaching us what mystics and indigenous people have always understood – that we are NOT separate, that the Universe is about connection, intimacy, diversity, and relationship. We are starting to wake up to the understanding that we ARE Earth, that we are the web of life, and that what we do to the air, water and soil of Earth, we do to our bodies and to each other.

Much has been given to us – and we are now called to use our uniquely human gifts to do nothing less than transform our entire species. Earth is counting on us to awaken to our true potential as conscious cosmic beings.

Each time I have a moment when I feel my deep oneness with all that is, each time I capture a fleeting glimpse of the unity of the universe, each time I know that we are not separate, I contribute to the growing consciousness that will lead to a new humanity. Whenever I touch into the reality of myself as Earth, as Universe, I know that I am moving the entire species forward in this transformation, and I have no doubt about the success of our endeavor. I know that we are on an exciting journey – one that began almost 14 billion years ago and has no intention of stopping.

The fact is those are still mostly fleeting moments. But as they happen more often and more powerfully, I am reminded that I will only be of service to the world by being fully awake to who I am – to the fact that I AM the planet – and by expanding my own consciousness and making space in myself to accept everything and everyone for wherever they are on the journey.

Albert Einstein said that we can't solve problems from within the same worldview in which they were created. The way forward is to look through new lenses – an expanded worldview, a new consciousness. It's a long process, and not one that can be accomplished by any one person. We are all in this together, yet our paths will be quite different.

My path has led me to ask many questions in my daily decision-making. When shopping, I am compelled to ask, "Where did this come from? How did it get here? How were the workers treated? Did its production cause any damage to Earth? Does its presence in my life make the world a better place?" Just as I want my life's work to contribute to the world, I want the things I buy and use to have a positive impact as well. Beyond the external choices of life, I know that I need to connect regularly with Earth – with ocean and beach, with trees and birds, with moon and stars – to nurture and support those fleeting moments of connection so that they may continue to grow and strengthen.

Some people touch into their awakening selves through meditation, some by gardening, some by walking in the woods, or spending time with children. Each time we each seek out these moments with intention, we wake up a bit more to the beauty and wisdom within, and we take our human family a step closer to our destiny as an integral part of a beautiful, sustainable, healthy planet.

"Namasté.
I honor the place in you where the whole universe dwells.
I honor the place in you which is of love, of truth, of light,
and of peace.
When you are in that place in you, and I am in that place in me,
We are One."

Gina Cawley has been inspired by Thomas Berry, Brian Swimme and the many wonderful people and creatures at Genesis Farm (www.genesisfarm. org). She currently coordinates eco-initiatives and sustainable business practices for the Conscious Corner, (www.rootsmkt.com) and is a fa-

cilitator of Awakening the Dreamer, Changing the Dream symposiums (www.awakeningthedreamer.org).

Answering the Call...
Making a Difference While
Doing What's Right for You

GINNY ROBERTSON

I am a recovering good girl. For the first 35 years of my life I did what others expected of me and lived up to their idea of who they thought I was. One of the things I did was volunteer. I volunteered because that is what good girls did. It didn't matter what the volunteer opportunity was. If someone asked me, I usually said yes. As a result, I got burned out and became resentful of those who asked and angry at myself for doing something I didn't want to do.

I also ended up doing things I didn't enjoy – like the time I became a Cub Scout den leader by default. Being surrounded by little boys who looked to me to give them something fun, entertaining and creative to do on a weekly basis was not my idea of a good time and it was very stressful. I also know that they weren't served as well by me as they would have been by someone who had a real desire to work with them.

I now believe that we should only volunteer to make a difference if it is something we are passionate about. We should take those things we love to do and find a way to use them in service to others. In making a difference we can contribute that which is most unique about us. We can act from our heart. I don't believe in selfless philanthropy. Personally, I don't think it exists. I think we should get tons from our volunteer efforts. We should, at the very least, feel better about ourselves for what we offer.

Like all of you, I am very busy. I run a business. I have a loving relationship with my husband that requires time and nurturing. I have a grown son I enjoy being with. I have friends and other family I want to connect with. And then there is the personal time I must have if I am to do my best in the world. So how do I have time for anything extra? How do I decide if and how to answer the call to serve?

I have come a long way since the days of being a Cub Scout leader. A number of things have changed to bring me to this place. First, I have released a lot of my attachment to what people think of me. The good girl doesn't show up nearly as much as she used to. And when she does I recognize her and her motives and gently ask her to step aside so that the real Ginny can be in charge. The second thing that has changed is that I now see service as an enhancement to my life, but not something I do blindly and selflessly. When offered an opportunity, I ask myself how being involved will add to my life and further my purpose for being on the planet. If it is a fit I look at how I will be able to use my gifts naturally and joyfully and truly benefit those in need of what I'm being asked to offer.

When I take the time to reflect and be sure that what I am being asked to do will fit with my life, just as it is, I can separate the needs of my ego from the needs of my soul. My ego still wants me to be the good girl and to do things that will enhance people's perception of me. My soul wants me to live on purpose and do things that feed me, knowing that others will be fed in the process. How do I know the difference? My ego speaks from my head and I think my way through it. My soul speaks from my heart and I feel my way through it.

It is interesting and important to note that the more I live from my soul the less I get asked to do. What happens is that I am awake and open to seeing where I can best serve so that when these opportunities arise I recognize them, get excited by the possibilities and take action. Since I trust my intuition and the creativity that comes out of that I know I am saying yes to something that will serve me as well as those I will be serving. And the really great news is that when I say yes from this place I give with ease and grace rather than struggle.

A living example of how this process has worked in my life is my involvement with the issue of mountaintop removal in my home state of West Virginia. This practice of blasting off up to 800 feet of the top of a mountain and flattening it, dumping the residue into valleys and streams and negatively impacting the quality of life for the residents has been going on since the 1980's. I was aware of the issue, but I wasn't losing any sleep over it. I just figured that the people there would deal with it the best they could. Even when a childhood friend ran for governor of the state and made mountaintop removal her main platform, I read about it with interest, but just didn't understand what it had to do with me.

In 2007 I was driving back to Baltimore from Asheville, North Carolina when I felt this overwhelming pull to take a detour and head to West Virginia, I couldn't shake the feeling so I trusted my gut and headed there. The short version of this story is that I found myself on a mountaintop removal site just minutes from where my childhood home had once been. What I saw was a vast wasteland that resembled pictures taken of the moon's surface. There were no trees, no grass, no birds, no insects. Nothing was alive. I stood outside my car for a while and the silence was unsettling. It wasn't until I got back in my car and headed down the mountain that I realized I had just been on a mountaintop removal site. I pulled over and wept.

At home I couldn't shake the images of what I had seen and I didn't know what to do about it. To say it haunted me would be an understatement. Four weeks later I was reading the weekly email from a local movie theatre and saw that a documentary about mountaintop removal was being shown the following week and that the filmmaker and some activists from West Virginia would be there. I contacted them, met them at the screening and then started looking for ways I could help get the word out about this practice. I didn't give a lot of thought to any of these actions before taking them. That is because I KNEW that I was supposed to do something. And I trusted that the something would reveal itself to me.

Since then, I have been responsible for over 1,000 people seeing this documentary and I continue to do what I can to shed light on this issue. I have used my gifts of connecting people, speaking and organizing to make a difference in a way that is natural to me. The look I see in people's eyes, the questions I hear them ask and the action I see them prepared to take after viewing this documentary feed me. I don't feel burdened by what I have added to my life and the time and energy it takes. I feel overjoyed by it.

This story could have had a very different outcome. My plate could have been so full with doing good girl things, that I wouldn't have heard my inner voice. I could have ignored the prompting that told me to change my route and head in another direction. Once there I could have driven by mindlessly and headed for home, wondering why I had gone in the first place. I could have opted not to read the email from the theatre. Or even if I had read it I could have chosen not to listen to what my heart was telling me. Even after seeing the documentary and meeting the women from West Virginia I could have decided not to get involved. But, you see, none of those were options. My soul was calling loudly and I had to answer the call.

"Everybody can be great... because anybody can serve. You don't have to have a college degree to serve. You don't have to make your subject and verb agree to serve. You only need a heart full of grace.
A soul generated by love."
MARTIN LUTHER KING, JR.

"Service to others is the rent you pay for your room here on earth."
MOHAMMED ALI

Ginny Robertson *is in the business of helping women live richer, fuller lives. She is a keynote speaker, founder of On Purpose Networking for Women, publisher of On Purpose Woman Magazine and the co-host of WomanTalk Live with Ginny Robertson & Ann Quasman, a weekly radio show. She also compiled the anthology The Spirit of Women Entrepreneurs: Real-Life Stories of Determination, Growth and Prosperity. She lives in Lutherville, MD with her Husband, Don. www.OnPurposeNow.com www.WomanTalkLive.com. Ginny invites you to learn more about mountaintop removal at blackdiamondsmovie. com and to see the documentary Black Diamonds: Mountaintop Removal and the Fight for Coalfield Justice by Catherine Pancake.*

$\mathcal{S}$TORY 42

Evolutionary Power: Transforming Organizations for Collaborative Success

CYNTHIA KING

I've been a peacemaker all my life. As the oldest of five children, I was the one who frequently stepped in to help resolve issues between my siblings. From there it was a natural progression to join the Peace Corps, work in a succession of social service positions, become a trained mediator, and seek partnerships anywhere I could find people interested in doing things in an alternative way. I so believe that when people are committed to coming together, there are ways to truly change the outcomes. Enter Evolutionary Women: I found members of my tribe!

I found that as Evolutionary Women, we are looking for ways to share our unique gifts and help to realize a world based on balance, equality, justice, harmony, and peace. We yearn for a community and a culture that supports those principles and sustains a healthy world that works for everyone, rather than a select few, and we are committed to co-creating that world. In the context of complex, disruptive social challenges and escalating environmental degradation, the stakes are high for creating deep, authentic collaboration to address those problems.

Yet many of us have felt especially stymied when we try to apply those evolutionary principles to the workplace. We have been particularly frustrated when we discover that internal power struggles and turf battles can disrupt even the most altruistic or "green" organizations, which then lose track of maintaining congruence between their outer missions and their inner relationships.

For example, I have recently had a particularly trying experience with an organization that has a beautifully articulate mission statement, programs that speak to my heart, and individuals who communicate many of the same values and goals that are priorities for me. I thought that because of these representative elements, this would be an organization that treats people with respect, keeps to their word, and operates on partnership principles. Unfortunately, that has not been my experience. I have been deeply disappointed to experience the same behaviors and treatment that I would have expected from a large, heartless corporation. In some way, since I had placed my trust in a certain expectation of how I would be treated by an organization that speaks to my heart, I feel betrayed.

I have also seen this same lack of congruence in small community groups, large corporations, international NGOs, and many government agencies. While resources shrink and countless organizations attempt to do more with less, bickering and competition increasingly limit the effectiveness of organizations of all sizes and types. The results of these disrupted interactions are costly, including lowered morale, reduced productivity, higher stress, and unwanted turnover.

As Evolutionary Women with a bright vision of how things could work, we often feel frustrated, confused, indignant, and angry when confronted by organizational barriers and traditions that keep so many of us stuck in dysfunctional relationship loops. Unfortunately, these obstructions are not an accident, nor are they necessarily due to a lack of skill or purpose. I have learned that they occur as the result of a fundamentally flawed operating system at the deep structure level of our culture and our organizations, which constantly undermines the evolutionary principles we prize. This operating system, based on a traditional hierarchy of power-over domination and control, disenfranchises many, and often stifles our voices while accumulating advantages for a privileged few.

Many of our organizations react to these situations by conducting "teambuilding" and "collaborative" initiatives, only to have them later fall apart when things get stressful and there is a lack of follow-up and support. In these situations, carefully constructed, lofty goals and change strategies seem foiled by forces beyond our control. Some react by instituting strict policies and procedures, hoping to stem the tide of conflict, and wishing that more tightly controlled interactions, policies, and operations might deliver greater predictability. What we fail to recognize is that unless the core operating system is transformed, it is difficult—if not impossible—for an organization to sustain desired changes for the long haul.

One of the stalemates in organizational change is an inherent tension between so-called "feminine" and "masculine" organizational styles and leadership behaviors, which gives a sense of having to choose directions between relationship building and productivity. The so-called "masculine" behaviors (which may be exhibited by both men and women) include action-oriented competition, individualism, pragmatism, intellectual prowess, maintaining control over one's emotions, and no-nonsense project completion—even at the expense of one's teammates.

This is "either-or" thinking at its best: either you have the power or you do not, and everyone is expected to constantly compete for more power and control. In the traditional system, these behaviors have been conventionally regarded as most desirable for leaders. While some are convinced that these "masculine" behaviors have been responsible for American successes, I believe that there is a serious lack of balance in this operating system. Furthermore, over-emphasis on those behaviors has resulted in significant losses, stemming from low morale, high turnover, and a grievance-prone workforce. It has also kept individuals and organizations in a tug-of-war, having to choose between two poles.

There is a complimentary set of so-called "feminine" behaviors (which also may be exhibited by both women and men). These behaviors include empathy, listening, compassion, collaboration, partnership, social cohesion and connectedness, inclusiveness, and valuing relationships. Particularly in the workplace, just as the "masculine" behaviors have been generally considered most desirable and productive, the "feminine" behaviors have often been considered weak and unproductive, or even detrimental. Yet these behaviors stem from "both-and" thinking: seeking to find the right balance between both action-oriented behaviors that produce and relationship-building ones that sustain.

Which set is really better? The answer is neither, at the exclusion or imbalance with the other. There are important aspects to be gleaned from each set, and most importantly, there is a deep need to rebalance all of these characteristics in both our cultural psyche and our organizations.

The good news is, there is an alternative organizational operating system, with viable, proven results in a wide variety of organizational contexts. This alternative system, the Partnership Model, is based on a view of power dynamics that completely reframes interpersonal and organizational interactions. This fundamentally different view of power involves the shared power of synergy, or power-with, rather than top-down control (power-over). At its core lie consideration of the common good and an emphasis on hearing from everyone involved in a system, along with striving for collaborative decision-making as much as possible. This kind of organization in turn requires a radically different style of leadership that leaves behind self-aggrandizing control, in exchange for seeking to be in service to others. It de-emphasizes competition and individual achievement, and emphasizes supporting and rewarding collective successes.

Here is a story about one of the organizations I have witnessed—and had the honor to work with—through their transformation from competitive hierarchies to co-creative, collaborative partnerships. This organization is the statewide unit of a Federal agency that made a collective, 180-degree turn, and moved from a traditional operating system to implementing the Partnership system. In spite of misunderstandings and many hurdles placed by their Washington headquarters, they now have over twelve years of a successful track record. They have phenomenal collaborative relationships with other agencies and local groups, and their morale, productivity, and retention have increased dramatically.

What made the difference? How did they do it? To begin with, they were led by an Evolutionary Woman (ahead of her time) with the vision to understand that a whole new way of doing business was possible, the courage to step outside the box, and the determination to steer the course through a myriad of barriers thrown up by individuals both inside and outside the organization. She exemplifies what many of us are seeking: the ability to balance and integrate select "masculine" and "feminine" leadership behaviors. She is action-oriented without relying on competition, and she certainly promotes and rewards intellectual achievement, along with all of the feminine behaviors mentioned above. Woven together, her balanced leadership provides inspiration, motivation, transformation, appreciation, and ultimately, cause for celebration.

She is the first to say that she did not accomplish this impressive feat alone. Even though there were some naysayers at the beginning, for the most part the organization's members have successfully demonstrated that when individuals are, in fact, freed from competition and strict hierarchies, they are collectively able to co-create sustainable practices. These practices include service, stewardship, and a web of alliances that, in turn, inform the values, ethics, structures, and policies of the organization. This kind of organizing requires a high level of self-awareness, a willingness to be vulnerable, and a readiness to engage in making the shift from traditional systems to a full-on partnership.

The Partnership principles that provided the foundation for that transformation offer a road map for all of us (in groups of all sizes) who seek to transform the ways we work together. They include:

1. Work toward inclusion, rather than promoting or even tolerating exclusion. Start by building relationships that consciously share power and influence, rather than allowing competition and control.
2. Place high value on practicing open, mutually respectful communication. Rather than dismissing difficulties as "just a communication problem," seek to upgrade communication skills and agreements all across the board. Include everyone in the organization—not just a few "problem children"—in learning new skills and setting new standards of truly collaborative behavior.
3. Accept and encourage other ways of knowing, learning, and contributing. Demonstrate recognition that wisdom comes from many sources by publicly acknowledging and honoring diverse perspectives and opinions.
4. Recognize both individual and team efforts. While it is good to recognize the "stars," it is also important to recognize and reward authentic teams and partnerships. Consistent recognition of collective efforts encourages more consistent collaboration.

When we look out at the problems of the world, or ponder the enormity of something like confronting and changing a fundamental operating system, we may feel small and limited in our effectiveness.

Yet by building a vision of what is possible, and working together to identify, effect, and sustain changes, we are a mighty force. This truth is beautifully expressed in this ancient Ethiopian proverb:

When spider webs unite, they can stop a lion.

Cynthia King, PhD *has been an organizational consultant for 30 years. She excels in guiding groups in transforming their working relationships and co-creating authentic collaboration and enduring partnerships. She also teaches about dialogue, collaboration, and reconciliation at Pacifica Graduate Institute. For more information on these concepts, see her book* Creating Partnerships: Unleashing Collaborative Power in the Workplace *(2005), available at www.creating-partnerships.com where the book's introduction is available as a free download. Cynthia can be reached at (805) 684-6844/P.O. Box 1055, Ventura, CA 93002.*

$\mathcal{S}$TORY 43

The Present

AMANDA KOH

There are many people who are discussing the benefits of living in the now – or the present moment. But, have you ever wondered what it actually feels like to be fully present? Is it even something we can define? In our traditional society, it seems that we have defined presence by our ability to actively perceive and remember what is happening around us. It is an easy judgment for our rational mind to assess. The connotations are one of an individual who is focused and aware, perhaps quick witted while engaged in a discussion, or focused on an activity, or fully absorbing a colorful sunset. All of these are wonderful states of being, indeed, but is being present something more?

It seems funny that I am even posing this question, as others rarely considered me to be present in my life. Even as a child, I was always the dreamer, lost in my thoughts, or my visions. I also seemed to have no concept of time or the need for efficiency or speed, in anything I ever did. As a child, my parents would inform me one hour before our departure anywhere, so I would have enough time to tie my shoes. My right shoe had to be as tight as physically possible, and my left - was so loose, there was barely any string left to make a bow. This dedication to my desired outcome simply took time.

In the evenings after school, my homework would take me the entire night. This being in the first grade, when other students spent about one half hour on their assignments. However, it wasn't that I was slow. I was simply methodical. Perhaps, I was actually comfortable, in simply being in the process and diving deep into the experience. This is what I wonder now.

In hindsight, I now understand the value in this single, slow speed. I understand the value in allowing the experience to expand, forgetting the concept of time. I believe my childhood holds the key to what allows presence to occur. And now, I know it is important for us to discuss our individual experiences of presence. I mean, when we are TRULY present. I believe we all experience it in our lives, even if only for a brief, fleeting moment.

The first time I remember feeling it was in college, at 18 years of age. I was attending an art school, studying Industrial Design, learning a wonderful way to sketch, with long, flowing lines. We would practice sketching lines that faded in from soft, become bold, and faded out to soft again as one graceful movement. Thick to thin, is what they called it. It was through this practice that I realized the art of the sketch itself – of the action of the sketch, rather than the product.

On this particular day, I had attended my furniture design class, and had images of potential coffee tables swirling around in my mind. I was excited to get back to the dorm rooms, where I would have an opportunity to begin sketching, and explore potential shapes. I walked with a couple of good friends to an apartment, and we all dropped our things and sat together on the couch. We were all very relaxed, and I sat in the middle, propping my legs up on the coffee table before me. I pulled out my masonite drawing board, setting it on my lap with some newsprint paper. Before me, I had several sharpened black Prismacolor pencils, so my "thick" could go to "thin" in every sketch. I was ready, and decided to change my position. I put my feet down, sat up straight and took a deep breath to focus on my activity. I don't remember talking - and I don't remember there being a TV in the room. Somehow, we were simply at peace with each other, and I began to sketch…

I put my pencil to the paper, and began to move it around, creating flowing lines and feeling my hand brush across the vanilla grey paper. I intended to explore shapes for a coffee table, but in that moment, I was focused more on the creation of the lines, and being open to letting them define the form. I continued to work like this for only a short time before it happened.

Within minutes of beginning, as I turned over a sheet of paper and began moving my hands once again, I felt this sudden sense of power rise within me. I remember my hands began to move in a rhythm all their own, as if they were in complete control. My hands, my arms, my body, all moved in effortless ability, and I watched as an elegant and strong form began to emerge. It was an amazing sensation – like nothing I had ever felt before. I was purely a witness to it. I watched as this beautiful drawing took shape, almost automatically. I had no thought to which way my hands would move, and I wouldn't have been able to create anything that perfect with thought if I had tried. And I believe that was the exact reason it had happened. I did not try to do anything. Instead, I let all of my expectations go.

When I finished the sketch, my jaw dropped open, as I perceived this beautiful organic form of a table I had drawn without preconception. The design was elegant and strong, with a gesture indicating forward and upward movement. The forms themselves were undulating and sinuous, similar to the natural patterns and rhythms of a weathered tree limb. And the design was created with the most gracefully bold thick to thin lines - the whole sketch glowing with soft, airy transitions from one line to another – indicative of a design drawn in one continuous movement.

That remains one of my favorite moments still, yet it was not the last time I felt such a sensation of flow. I have been blessed to experience this sensation nearly ten times in my life since, and have had wonderful moments, which extended for even longer periods of time. Through this, I know I have the ability to sense and Be so much more around me. I say Be more around me, because in those moments, I expand. I let go of my mind's limitations, and I feel my being as far more expansive than my physical body.

I also know, the more I bring myself to activities which focus these relaxed and open energies, the more opportunity I will have to fall into this state. I say this because that is what it feels like. It feels like I am finally releasing my hold on this perception and falling away. Yet, I do not fall down. I fall Up. My judgments fall away, and my Spirit Rises.

I now know that my thinking mind, which perceives our world of words and time, holds my attention, and only a part of my Presence. It limits the fullness I can otherwise experience. When my thinking mind is dominant, I am being captivated by a world through binoculars. Yet, in these amazing experiences, I have dropped the tunneling tool before my eyes, and realized the vast expanse in my periphery all around. When I do this, is when I become fully Present. And I believe the Present is the Now in which we are all meant to be.

I must share with you, however, one word of caution. Beware of the desire to experience this state. The desire will only serve to prevent the shift from occurring. Be joyful, relaxed and focused on the task in the moment, and know that you are Being everything you are right Now. Then forget that you are Being anything. Live. Breathe. Feel. Do what you love. Intend your goal, then focus on creating the lines. Forget the sketch. The goal will draw itself.

Why do I tell you this? Frankly, as I am writing this, I wonder myself. I do know of some reasons. For one, I wonder how many other people have felt something similar. I wonder for those who have felt a sudden shift in their energy and abilities, what brings you into that state? I do believe many, if not all people, experience something like this in their lifetime, but I know it is not an everyday experience. Yet, it is an amazing experience. And because of this, I mostly wonder - why do we discuss this so rarely?

I believe it is time to discuss what we each experience when we are in the Present moment, because I sense this is a vital part of who we are, and who we are becoming. This moment - when we are experiencing this expanded awareness and capability, may be exactly what all of our religions have been attempting to describe. It is time we understand the message they have been attempting to deliver.

What is it that our religions have been seeking to help us understand? What is enlightenment? Is enlightenment this state of being fully aware and engaged? Could it be possible, that we may all begin to be in this space more often, and for longer periods of time? May we come to be in this space always? What would be possible, if we all experienced our Present, simultaneously? Could this be our new Awakening? Could this Gift be our coming Consciousness?

Amanda Koh *is an artist living in the beautiful Pacific Northwest region of North America. In addition to her work as a Digital Sculptor, she also paints the Horse, with which she has always been connected. Her fluid and ethereal paintings of horses are admired by many, and much of her art is shared through a unique method she calls Art Caretaking. For more information, please visit her website at: www.amandakoh.com*

Women and Deeksha: Empowering Humanity with the Feminine Presence

CHARLENE M. PROCTOR, PH.D.

Margaret Thatcher once said that a woman's mission is not to enhance the masculine spirit, but to express the feminine. "Hers is not to preserve a man-made world," she said, "but to create a human world by the infusion of the feminine element into all of its activities." This means practicing life from a balanced point of view by aligning with a uniquely feminine set of values, such as community building. We never wanted to create a man's world (we forgot about cooperation in the corporate scurry of the eighties) but instead yearn to demonstrate our core beliefs through a full-blown rendition of our authentic selves. This is the Sacred Feminine principle, which is love and the primary teacher of relationship. All life is one form of relationship or another and women know we are cosmic connectors capable of making peace between nations as well as our darling offspring.

Revisiting our spiritual roots highlights our ability to uplift human consciousness by a single thought or touch that transmits the power of Grace, our primary connection resolving all inner conflicts. Because most women have a natural awareness of the well-being of entire systems, they can integrate unity consciousness into their work while deepening their relationship with the Divine Presence. Humans are rapidly opening up to this natural gift through deeksha, an energetic transmission that initiates the awakening of a person into a state of oneness, or unity with God. Since the Feminine is the embodiment of heart energy, and giving and receiving deeksha is an intuitive activity, women are on the threshold of empowering humanity by communion with the Divine and initiating this experience in others.

Deeksha, or what is becoming known as The Oneness Blessing, ™ is the process of transferring divine grace bringing about a shift in human consciousness. It activates a neurobiological change in the brain that supports awakening, slows the senses down, and frees the sense from the constant chatter of the mind. It dissolves our perception of separation and results in more clarity and feelings of love and joy. Now being transmitted from one person to another by both spiritual masters and initiates through touch, intention, or glance, it satisfies the natural longing for inclusion, receptivity, and relationship. The separate "me" is no longer in charge. It is a shift from ego to essence, changing an individual's outlook and reality.

Women are on the verge of moving humanity forward because they are acutely aware of the energetic balance needed to evolve consciousness. Women are weary of approaching life purely from the Mind because they honor the internal process. Relying exclusively upon the head has been a source of depression, fatigue, and illness for the feminine spirit. Mind represents a somewhat masculine idea seated in structure, left brain logic, mechanistic and lineal problem-solving activities, control, planning, and science (often without morality and common sense). It's exactly what we need to unplug from more often and surrender to the inclusion of the present moment, to the unfettered feminine rendition of life. Humanity is hungering to feel life moving through their being, which is a natural, inherent feminine perspective.

Years ago, I began my own awakening when I visited Her Holiness Sai Maa Lakshmi Devi to receive a similar blessing of grace. Sai Maa was heralded in many spiritual circles as one of the great masters of our time, reputed to be responsible for numerous healings. Her teachings are broad and flavored with an interfaith attitude of inclusion, scooping up congregants from many flocks. (She says the next new religion will be love.) Sai Maa's deeksha and Samskara Shuddhi, the process of clearing negative emotional patterns from the body's energetic fields, can transform anyone in her presence. After a friend convinced me to look her up on the Internet, I could feel her Shakti buzzing through my fingers on the keyboard into my body. I knew I needed to see her.

Lining up for a Hindu-style blessing is something the Western mind has trouble processing. Darshan is the spiritual energy blessing received by an individual while in the presence of a holy person; deeksha is the actual energy transfer. You don't walk up to Sai Maa to receive deeksha. You line up behind hundreds, with an offering of flowers or photographs, and wait at least three hours while continuously chanting. The last hundred yards or so you crawl on your knees. The guru-master is one who is fully attuned to the Divine Presence and constantly radiates grace. As a teacher, a guru represents embodied Spirit and symbolizes devotion to God, one who has achieved mastery.

By the time I ascended to the podium on darshan day, I had chanted about a thousand Kyrie Eleisons - a Gregorian litany favorite of Roman Catholics. Literally, the Greek translation is "Lord have mercy; Christ have mercy; Lord have mercy." This, in addition to "Sh'ma Yisrael Adonai eloheinu Adonai ekhad" ("Hear O Israel, the Lord our God, the Lord is One") and dozens of Sanskrit chants, did not prepare me for the outpouring of love when I first laid my head in the lap of Her Holiness. Her energy showered me like a harmonic rain, triggering an emotional downpour. It felt like coming home.

When love moves in, it recognizes what little you already have, and plugs the holes in your heart-sieve so you are no longer wasting but dispensing it to fortify yourself against darkness. Past emotional attire evaporates - like fear, self-doubt, and worry- leaving you naked in the truth of who you are. I could not stop crying after returning to my chair. My friend Sandy leaned over and wrapped her arms around me. "When we are in the presence of complete and unconditional love," she whispered, "it is overwhelming."

It's true. Being in God's presence, whether it is the guru's rendition of Divine love or by holding a baby, begins to fully open us to the magnificence of a unified universe. We are suddenly astounded by the ultimate relationship of simplicity and power; our empathy and willingness to serve is amplified. When invited, pure love washes you squeaky clean. When I got up the next morning, I still felt Maa rocking me in a comforting, rhythmic embrace. I was superbly washed, dried, and folded. She did this for five hundred people that day, all of them invited to open up to their potential. Our only choice was to kindly ask all pain to move over and leave. There was no room left, except for love.

I realized women are here to demonstrate love in action and sing a natural song of co-creation from this energy vortex that resides in the middle of our chests. Deeksha begins to move us from living in the "what should be" to the "what is." In a moment, the sum total of everything negative we have ever believed about ourselves is scrubbed. Suddenly we're safe in All There Is. We never really left because our Source is perfect and so are we.

While Sai Maa held my face in her hands, she said that she had finally found me and told me I was a beautiful soul. "You will manifest great works," she said. I thanked her and knelt, lowering my forehead to the ground in front of her feet. The gesture means our heart center should always remain higher than our head. When we recognize the Divine in the guru, humbled by love around us, in us, as us, or in anyone else for that matter, we see it in ourselves. Remembering our oneness is how we become God.

In the following years I received deeksha from many spiritual masters and initiates, it was always the same: only peace and clarity remained, and an attunement to reality. When we allow grace to enter us, it chases away feelings of loneliness, despair, dryness, insecurity, and discouragement. Grace feels like the Mother, the feminine presence. It's the comfort we miss. To surrender to it without resistance is the end of personal suffering.

Since then, I have often thought about the passage "The works that I do shall you do also; and greater works than these you shall do," which sounded like what Maa said to me that day. If there is anything that will awaken you to your own potential it is these words because everyone, master or student, must turn inside out at some point and have a closer look at how to better approach life, purging negative patterns or past emotional baggage. Awareness flowers in the "what is" and not "what should be." And truth in the form of an energetic touch can ignite compassion from our deepest well where purity represents the holy unity of all things: one consciousness birthed in matter and light synthesized where feminine wisdom exists.

I've carried Sai Maa's love around for nearly four years now, anchoring the divine qualities within, cementing them into my very being. To be a healing presence for humanity means consciously touching the world with empowering wisdom. This rebirth of the light within each one of us will build a foundation for a new reality that embodies the heart of God. Grace passed on as a simple blessing can inspire us to be conduits for the human experience, as long as we are open to its magnificence.

Charlene M. Proctor, Ph.D., *Founder of The Goddess Network, is the best-selling author of* Let Your Goddess Grow! 7 Spiritual Lessons on Female Power and Positive Thinking *and* The Women's Book of Empowerment: 323 Affirmations that Change Everyday Problems into Moments of Potential. *A certified Oneness Blessing facilitator and a Minister of Spiritual Peacemaking, she is dedicated to helping awaken individuals from all walks of life to the magnificence of their own Divine gifts.*

The Afterword

BONNIE KELLEY

Imagine lying on your back on a warm sunny day, the blanket beneath you soft, padding your fully extended body as muscles twitch to relieve routine tensions. Think of closing your eyes and fully stretching out your fingers and toes—wiggle them for a moment, feel the wonder of your extremities. Settle in further, breathe gently, drop deeper into restfulness. Ever-so-slowly become aware of the sweet, surrounding breeze, let it tenderly tickle the surface areas of your skin, and now take another breath.

Turn your head. Appreciate the shade of the nearby tree. Take note that the lofty branches span with thick leaves, splendid in their diffusing the noontide sun. Hmmm, do you hear a distant buzz? Never mind, only harmless insects hovering. And now, what's that? Can you smell something pleasing? A light flowery scent is wafting from the play of wild flowers you hadn't noticed until just now, adorning the field. Ah, yes, life is good. Take another breath and let out a sigh, appreciating the stillness. Stretch your attention one more moment, dare to whisper with me: I feel safe in this place.

If you have made it thus far, thank you for traveling to the "Afterword" experience with me.

What I most want to convey in this finishing piece is the feeling of what it has meant to be involved in the conscious choices of this book project: *Conscious Choices: An Evolutionary Woman's Guide to Life.*

Together with my Evolutionary Women's collective, over a period of several months, we 40 or so women crafted our individual stories, and along with the help of a 100 +others who actively witnessed the process, we gave birth to a new function that is showing up as "a feminine field of freedom." Besides assembling this book, we literally wrote into existence a place of acceptance. What we've come to think of as our back lot experience continues to issue forth unique forms of out-picturing, which I unselfconsciously proclaim are transcendent marvels.

These sweet petals of spaciousness circled together into a full blown identity that grew out of a plethora of desires, strengths, longings, difficulties, needs, personal gifts and resources. We co-created this environment of appreciation using a colorful collection of quirky styles and tones —we blossomed surprisingly from what might be described as natural substrate.

Mysteriously, the potential for this emerging design seems to have waited for the perfect set of conditions to make its appearance. This very visibility generated itself repeatedly as accruing mutuality got stronger and more defined each day. It invited us in (actually, we invited ourselves in because we volunteered to write the stories). Then miraculously, the energy itself saw to it that the increasing richness flowed out, which promptly attracted more like-hearted attributes to reveal themselves, and in return the mutuality wove itself back into varied wholeness.

Practical application took the guise of what we lovingly referred to as "gentle readers." These women reviewed each story and shared their peer guidance by reflecting how much they liked, what specifics needed more clarification—and finally, tender suggestions were thoughtfully laid out for editing purposes. We held weekly teleconference calls, which many of the women tuned into, and even if they didn't, they reported a palpable sense of resonance cheering them on. An abundance of emails flew freely between various individuals and many of these were read by all.

What revealed itself from the unfolding sequence, along with the book in your hands, is a multi-faceted human tapestry. It appears we initiated an experiential weaving process that used us as the colorful strands, each bringing in our own particular human gifts and resources, until finally the traits converged and transformed into a coherence. Starting off with singular actions our engagement process spread its wings exponentially and by the end we had morphed into a community of flying women. The warm drafts lifted us even higher when we realized we had morphed into major pieces of The Actual Creation—instead of being mere participants.

You might think I'm exaggerating but I assure you this was an organic arising. We simply followed our innate attraction to bonding and the group sensitivity grew to heights none of us had experienced before. We were a synchronized species who suddenly recognized deep intimacy revealing itself during the flow of our actions; in this case we discovered an immense sense of synergy.

We basked in a realm of continual acceptance and appreciation. I've struggled to find a simple explanation for this phenomenon and my truth is I believe that we were resonating to a divine emanation. I'm taking a leap of faith to go to this extreme, I agree. And yet, though it might sound presumptuous, my gut says, "We became a heavenly attunement." In a conference conversation one night, Pamela, a woman from Arkansas stated with her usual grace, "I am grounded in the unknown," and all eight of us shared that we felt that way too. Agreement of this nature was our norm.

It is worth noting here, however, that mutuality doesn't hoard its riches. Quite the contrary. Resonance multiplies out resolutely to touch the sensibilities of countless other Pamelas and Marilyns and Anne Franceses and LaVonnes, and Megans who are ready in the world, similarly inclined to voice their truths.

Our love profited from this evolving intimacy and it spawned many healthy beginnings. With no abrupt endings that I recall. I honestly don't remember rigidity coming into form. Judgmental, narrow minded, restrictive energy would not have survived this field.

An assortment of women showed up, and in our willingness to describe life's deepest desires and priorities, we unearthed (or were unleashed, I should say!), a penchant for feminine potential. Evolutionary writings have now been consciously gathered; we are here en masse, claimed by it. The die is cast. Evolutionary eyes are focused to see the Divine, as the Divine.

Beyond the monologic of any one metaphor, we know convergence, and our spiritual footprints are everywhere, from the eight directions—no place left out. May these writings continue to make their way, as a kind of field guide for those to come.

Beyond seeking, you have already joined the field. Welcome. Breathe the open air, remembering Rumi's promise:

"Beyond the realms of right and wrong there is a field
I will meet you there"

Bonnie Kelley is the co-founder of Evolutionary Women. She serves humanity in several areas of creative expression: product development, networking, writing, inspirational speaking, fundraising, promotion, community organization, group facilitation and educational outreach. Her most beloved endeavor is to "illuminate the circuitry" which according to Bonnie means to facilitate the process of connecting the enlightened aspects of human kind. She has one daughter, Sara, who is married to Jeff, and they have 2 children, Maddy and Vinnie. Bonnie loves being a grandmother.

An Invitation to Evolutionary Women!

Evolutionary Women is an organization dedicated to empowering women who are committed to co-creating, with all of humanity, a world that works for everyone. We hope you'll join us.

Here's how you can get involved:

3 Things Every Woman Should Know about the Future – Free Audio

This positive and inspiring recorded discussion of the future by the three founders of Evolutionary Women outlines the great potential for our planet and the significant role that women are playing to realize our highest aspirations

www.EvolutionaryWomen.org/ccaudio

Evolutionary Women Retreats

Give yourself the empowering gift to come to one of our 3-day retreats that bring together women who are committed to their own personal development, the larger human family, and our Planet.

It is in the rich, embracing environment of Evolutionary Women retreats that women birth new ideas within themselves, partner with other like-minded individuals and form new circles of connection that enhance your lives and further your missions.

www.EvolutionaryWomen.org/retreats

Become a Member of Evolutionary Women

As a member of Evolutionary Women you'll be supported in your emergence of the new archetype, the Feminine Co-Creator. You will be part of an expanding community that is committed to peace, global cooperation and co-creation.

- Receive a FREE subscription to the Evolutionary Women newsletter including tips, tools and stories to help you embrace the lifestyle of an Evolutionary Woman.
- Receive invitations to conferences and events with teachers, writers and activists on the evolutionary edge of their fields
- Get FREE audio downloads, teleclasses and more
- Contribute to scholarships to our events for women in need

www.EvolutionaryWomen.org/membership

Also by Love Your Life Publishing

The Freedom Formula: How to Put Soul in Your Business and Money in Your Bank
Christine Kloser

The MavHERick Mind: How to Win the Battle for Success by Using What You've Got to Get What You Want
Liz Pabon

The Spirit of Women Entrepreneurs: Real-Life Stories of Determination, Growth and Prosperity
Ginny Robertson

Power and Soul: 42 Successful Entrepreneurs Share Their Secrets for Creating the Business and Life of your Dreams
Alexandria Brown

Conscious Entrepreneurs: A Radical New Approach to Purpose, Passion and Profit
Christine Kloser

Learn more about these and other
Love Your Life Publishing books:

Love Your Life
Love Your Life Publishing
PO Box 2
Dallastown, PA 17313
(800) 930-3713
www.LoveYourLifeBooks.com